Elegant Glass Candle Holders

Brilliant Cut Era, Roaring '20s, Depression Era, Modern

Paula Pendergrass and Sherry Riggs

Schiffer Publishing Ltd

4880 Lower Valley Road, Atglen, PA 19310 USA

Dedication

This book is dedicated to our collectors who made this book possible by letting us into their homes and becoming our friends.

Library of Congress Control Number: 2002100926

Designed by "Sue"
Type set in ZapfHumanist Dm BT/Korinna BT

ISBN: 0-7643-1635-4
Printed in Hong Kong
1 2 3 4

Published by Schiffer Publishing Ltd.
4880 Lower Valley Road
Atglen, PA 19310
Phone: (610) 593-1777; Fax: (610) 593-2002
E-mail: Schifferbk@aol.com
Please visit our web site catalog at
www.schifferbooks.com
We are always looking for people to write books on new and related subjects. If you have an idea for a book, please contact us at the above address.

This book may be purchased from the publisher.
Include $3.95 for shipping.
Please try your bookstore first.
You may write for a free catalog.

In Europe, Schiffer books are distributed by
Bushwood Books
6 Marksbury Avenue
Kew Gardens
Surrey TW9 4JF England
Phone: 44 (0) 20 8392 8585
Fax: 44 (0) 20 8392 9876
E-mail: Bushwd@aol.com
Free postage in the UK. Europe: air mail at cost.

Acknowledgments

Collectors and Consultants

Tom Bloom, C.J. Bodensteiner, Jackie Brown, Mrs. Mary Buzzell, Mr. and Mrs. Horace Dickens, Joy Griggs, Bill and Diane Haight, Hanley and Margaret Jennings, Kathleen Kelley, Sim and Betty Lucas, Bob and Shirley Maruca, Robert Meador and Armando Ramirez, Mr. and Mrs. Wayne Phillips, Janet and Dale Rutledge, Cheryl Sedlar, Aldona Standridge, Matzi and Jeff Thrasher, Mary Ann and Jay Thielen, Rodney, Ann and Davis Tillman, David Vance, Enid and Len Waska, Mary Lee Wilson (IGS), and Julie Zoller.

Malls, Businesses and Dealers

Bloom's Charles Street Antiques, Wellsburg, West Virginia; Crown Antiques, Russellville, Arkansas; Han-Mar's Odd Shop, Weslaco, Texas; J.T. Texas, Tomball, Texas; Olde Tyme Treasures, Little Rock, Arkansas; Sherry Riggs Antiques, Houston, Texas; Sisters 2 Too, Alma, Arkansas; The Antique Company Mall, McKinney, Texas; Southwest Antiques, Houston, Texas; Tillman's Antiques & Collectables, Hot Springs, Arkansas; and We Love Antiques, Dover, Arkansas.

Technical Support

Bill Belovicz; Ken Riggs; Bob Maruca; Mark and Bridgitt Ussery: Express Foto, Russellville, Arkansas.

Editorial Support

The Schiffer Publishing Group and its staff; Peter Schiffer; and our editor, Donna Baker.

Contents

Introduction

What is elegance but a combination of line, form, and decoration that announces the unquestionable taste and skill of the designer and master craftsman? What is charm, but the blend of color, shape, and decoration that delights the eye and sparks a whimsical memory of good times past? In this book we showcase both elegance and charm by including candle holders with exquisite engravings from the Brilliant Cut Glass era, candle holders with rich colors and detailed silver and gold overlays from the Roaring '20s, candle holders with elaborate etchings from the Depression era, and modern candle holders from both the United States and Europe that demonstrate the skill and creativeness of twentieth century glass makers. What follows is a survey of the richness of style, color, and character in glass candle holders that epitomizes glass making at its best.

Identification of candle holders in this book is based on publications, catalogs, manufacturer's verification, manufacturers' marks, and affixed labels. **Pricing** is based on publications, mall prices, glass show prices, and advice from expert collectors and dealers. Although our pricing research is comprehensive, it is not foolproof; it cannot account for regional differences, nor can it predict future trends. Prices are given as a suggested range for mint condition items, with the upper price being for the most desirable colors and/or treatments. **Important**: In this book, where many rarer and more expensive candle holders are featured, a pair will be worth more than twice the price of a single and a signature will increase the value by 20-30%.

Candle holders are listed alphabetically by manufacturer or known retailer. Foreign candle holders are listed by country with the manufacturer also being identified, if known. The progression in each section is from shorter to taller, and from single, to double, to triple, etc.; however, similar candle holders have been grouped by line number or by style in some places.

All measurements in this book are actual measurements of the candle holder shown, not catalog listings. **A word of caution**: candle holders from the same line commonly vary $\pm$ 0.5 inch, so a candle holder described in the literature as being 3" could be as short as 2.5" while another one could be as tall as 3.5". (Here's a **tip** from Sim Lucas: "If you don't have a tape [measure], you can use a dollar bill which is 6" long on the button!")

A **bobeche** is a ring placed or molded around the base of the light; prisms are generally attached. For consistency, we have used the term **candelabra** to refer to holders with bobeches and prisms attached. The term **lustre** refers to candle holders with a fixed bobeche or with prisms suspended from the globe area; a **nappy** is a candle dish with a handle; an **epergne** is a vase that fits into the light in place of a candle. An **etching** is a roughened surface pattern usually created by sandblasting or application of acid; a **cutting** is engraved into the glass with a sharp instrument; a **puntie** (or **punty**) is a polished rounded or oval indentation.

Candle Holders and Their Values

Beaumont Company

Morgantown, West Virginia, early 1900s-1962. Tableware, boudoir items, and lighting.

Beaumont 2" x 5" #148 hexagonal rolled edge single light candle holder. Cobalt with silver deposit: $90-95 pair; black with decoration: $80-85 pair. Probably made in pink and green. (c. 1920s-1930s). **Fostoria's** #2375 ° 'Fairfax' is a similar mold with a much larger base.

Beaumont 4.5" single light candle holder. Fer-lux (opaque white with semi-transparent look): $80-85 pair; ruby, cobalt: $95-100 pair. (c. 1920s-mid 1930s). **Note**: fer-lux was discontinued in 1936.

Beaumont close-up of silver deposit.

Beaumont 5.25" x 4.25" single light candle holder. Fer-lux with platinum trim, ruby, cobalt, decorated fer-lux: $95-100 pair; crystal: $65-70 pair; plain fer-lux: $75-80 pair.

Beaumont 8.5" single light candle holder with optic pattern. Crystal with blue and black enamel background and gold and white enamel decoration on outer surface: $185-200 pair. Can be found in crystal optic with various enameled decorations including 'Charlton.' (c. 1920s). Note the optic pattern on this stick; compare with **Tiffin** #151. We are placing this candle holder here with some reservation. **U.S. Glass** did make an optic pattern table service; however we cannot document this candle holder as one of theirs.

Beaumont close-up of decoration.

Beaumont alternate view of decoration.

Beaumont 3.5" x 11" x 3.75" triple light candle holder with heavy silver edges and etched cameos with roses and floral baskets. Blue, green: $225-250 pair; crystal satin: $200-225 pair. Blue and light green may have been made in satin.

Belgium

Cristalleries du Val Saint-Lambert, 1826-present. Brilliant cut glass, including both finished products and blanks. Leader in cased glass, both overlay and triple layer.

Left:
Belgium (Val St. Lambert) 9" single light candlestick. Crystal with crystal satin floral design: $400-450 pair. Marked.

Right:
Belgium (Val St. Lambert) 11.75" #1/14566 chandelier with hexagonal base and light. Crystal with heavy cutting: $750-800 pair. Shown in 1908 Val St. Lambert ACGA catalog.

Beaumont close-up of etching.

Far left:
Belgium (Val St. Lambert) 10.75" single light candlestick with four eagles. Crystal satin: $650-700 pair. Signed.

Left:
Belgium (Val St. Lambert) alternate view.

Cambridge Glass Company

Cambridge, Ohio, 1902-1958. Tableware, dinnerware, and occasional pieces of all kinds. The molds were sold to **Imperial Glass Corporation** in 1960.

Cambridge 2.25" #1155 'Springtime' three-footed single light candle bowl. Jade (light emerald green satin), rose du barry (peach-blo satin): $80-85 pair; krystol (crystal satin): $60-65 pair; cinnamon (amber satin): $75-80 pair; mystic (willow blue satin): $85-90 pair. (c. 1930). **Note**: only the pattern sides of 'Springtime' pieces were satinized.

Cambridge alternate view.

Cambridge 3" #628 variant single light candle holder. Dark amethyst with #725 plate etching and gold trim: $60-65 pair; peach-blo: $55-60 pair. (c. 1930s). Note the ball-like column ring.

Cambridge close-up of #725 etching.

Below:
Cambridge 3.625" #628 single light candle holder. Crystal with #752 'Diane' etching: $45-50 pair. Note the wafer-like column ring.

Below right:
Cambridge 4" #66 'Krystolshell' or #SS66 'Coral' single light footed dolphin candle holder. Crown tuscan: $245-260 pair; also listed as #66 'Krystolshell' in forest green with a crystal base: $150-160 pair; and as #66 'Sea Shell' in crystal: $100-110 pair. (c. 1940s-1950s).

Cambridge 4" #1502 flower/candle frog in #235 rose bowl with two 5" #68 (same as '#68 Cascade' made 1949-1950s) 'Caprice' single light candle holders. Crystal candle holders (1953-1954): $35-40 pair; crystal rose bowl (c. 1936-1945): $85-90 each; moonlight blue flower/candle frog: $70-75 each. Total value: $190-205.

Cambridge 4.875" #1617 'Martha' single light hurricane base. Crystal with #772 'Chantilly' etching and #D/1060 gold edge decoration: $95-100 pair; complete with 5" etched chimney: $600-650 pair. (c. 1936-1958).

Cambridge close-up of #772 'Chantilly' etching and #D/1060 gold edge.

Cambridge 6.625" x 4.5" #68 line #3797 or #3797/68 'Square' two-piece hurricane lamp. Crystal: $100-110 pair; with ebony base: $110-120 pair. (c. 1949-mid 1950s). Reissued by **Imperial** in regal ruby: $120-130 pair.

Cambridge 5.375" #66 'Nearcut' single light four-sided candlestick. Crystal with horizontal bands and corner cuts, ebony: $90-95 pair; azurite: $95-100 pair. (c. 1920s-1930s). Also made in 7" #67 'Nearcut'.

Cambridge 6" 'Twist' single light candle holder. Royal blue, all transparent colors: $95-100 pair; opaque colors: $85-90 pair. (c. 1931-1940). Two-part mold; **U.S. Glass** has a similar three-part mold. Also comes in 8.5".

Cambridge 7" #70 'Caprice' single light candle holder. La Rosa with alpine accent, moonlight blue with alpine: $150-160 pair; crystal with alpine: $75-80 pair. (c. 1936-1954).

Cambridge 'Caprice' console set with 7" #70 candle holders and #65 11" four-footed, two-handled bowl. La Rosa with alpine accent: $275-295 set.

Cambridge 7.25" #70 'Caprice' single light candle holder. Moonlight blue, la rosa; $150-160 pair; crystal: $70-75 pair. Notice the blue prism.

Cambridge 7.125" #72 or #200-20 'Nearcut' single light, six-sided candle holder with pressed rays under base. Heliotrope, ivory, primrose: $85-90 pair; crystal, azurite, ebony, jade: $75-80 pair. May command a higher price with cuttings, etchings, or decorations.

Cambridge 7.375" #71 or #200/6 'Nearcut' or #2800/235 'Community' single light candle holder. Heliotrope, primrose: $85-90 pair; azurite, ebony, jade, crystal: $75-80 pair. May command a higher price with cuttings, etchings, or decorations. (c. 1920s-1930s).

Left:
Cambridge 7.5" #69 or 200/2 'Nearcut' single light candle holder. Ivory, heliotrope, primrose: $85-90 pair; crystal, ebony, azurite, jade: $75-80 pair; carrara (opaque white opalescent): $125-135 pair. May command a higher price with cuttings, etchings, or decorations. **Note**: made in opaque colors only except for crystal. Also made in 10" as #68.

Right:
Cambridge 7.5" #200/18 or #2862 'Nearcut' single light candle holder. Transparent colors: mulberry, emerald, light emerald green: $75-80 pair; amber, crystal: $65-70 pair; opaque colors: heliotrope, jade, primrose: $85-90 pair. This candle holder was made for deep etchings, cuttings, and engravings, and the price will be higher accordingly. (c. 1903-1930). It is listed as being 7" in various catalogs; it also comes in 6" and 6.5". **Paden City** and **Duncan** made similar candle holders. The **Paden City** candle socket is thicker; the bulge in the stem is in a lower position in the **Duncan** candle holder.

Cambridge 7.5" 'Column' single light candle holder. Crystal with sea foam green paint and floral decoration: $25-30 pair. Probably purchased from **Cambridge** and decorated by another company. Has an old price sticker of $1.50 pair. (c. 1920s).

Cambridge 7.5" 'Column' single light candle holder. Rubina with green dominance: $230-250 pair; cobalt 2, ritz blue: $90-95 pair; amber, crystal, crystal satin: $65-70 pair. (c.1925-1940). **Note**: Most Rubina sticks have a dominance of one of three colors: blue, green, or red. Also found in 7" and 9.25". Rubina is rare.

Cambridge 9.5" 'Column' single light candle holder. Ivory (opaque cream), primrose, jade: $100-110 pair; avocado, ebony: $110-120 pair; azurite, heliotrope: $120-130 pair. Also comes in transparent colors and in 7.5" and 8.5" heights.

Cambridge 8.25" x 4.5" single light 'Twist' candle holder. Mulberry, topaz, light emerald: $100-110 pair. **Note**: this is a two-part mold; **U.S. Glass** used a three-part mold.

Cambridge 9.5" #65 'Doric Column' single light candle holder. Ivory, azurite, ebony, jade (all with gold trim): $165-175 pair; heliotrope with gold: $175-185 pair; carrara with gold: $260-275 pair. (c. 1920s-1930s).

Cambridge 'Twist' console with 8.25" single light candle holders and 9.5" bowl. Jade, additional opaque colors: candle holders: $90-100 pair; $135-150 set.

Cambridge 9.25" #65 'Doric Column' single light candle holder with 9.25" 'Ramshead' bowl. Heliotrope with heavy silver trim. Candle holders: $175-185 pair; bowl: $200-225 each.

Left:
Cambridge 9.5" #109 'Dolphin' single light candle holder. Peach blo, light emerald green, forest green: $325-350 pair; amber: $185-195 pair; emerald green, Mandarin gold: $350-375 pair; ivory: $450-500 pair; cobalt 2: $500-550 pair; rubina (rare): $1250-1500 pair. (Amber: c. 1955-1958; all others: c. 1925-1930). Four-part mold.

Right:
Cambridge 9.625" #1 'Crucifix' single light candle holder. 1903 Catalog: 'Opal Novelties' white milk glass: $225-250 pair; 1910 Catalog: 'Nearcut' crystal: $175-200 pair.

Cambridge close-up of figure.

Cambridge 9.625" #1 'Crucifix' single light candle holder. Turquoise: $225-250 pair. This color has not been documented for this stick; however, Cambridge did produce a limited quantity of turquoise, and this may have been a special order. Turquoise and opal were listed in the 1903 catalog; both were discontinued by 1906.

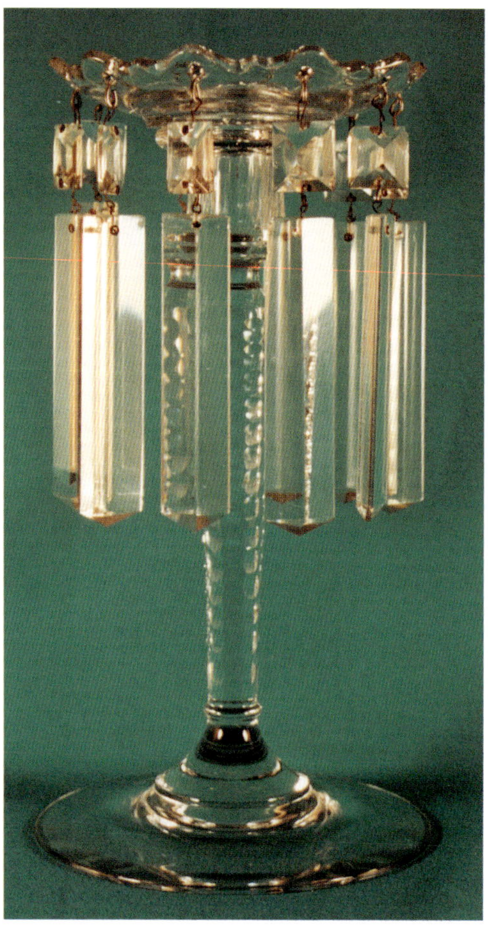

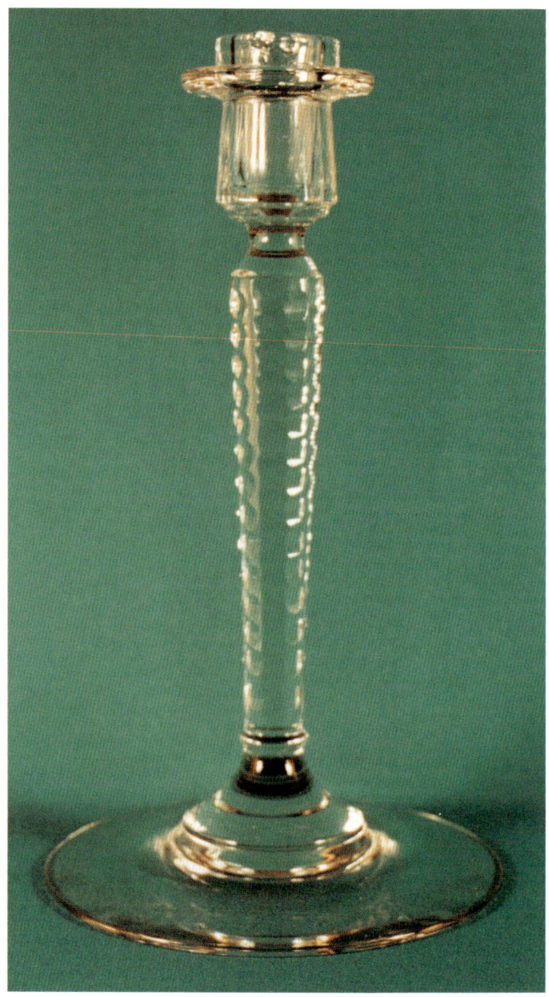

Right:
Cambridge 9.75" #1272 single light candle holder with #20 oversize locking bobeche and ten 'C' prisms (5"). Crystal: $450-500 pair. (c. 1930s-1940s).

Far right:
Cambridge alternate view showing fire polished cuttings. Crystal: $300-325 pair. Produced in pastels without a bobeche lip as #636.

Cambridge 5.125" #1603 keyhole single light hurricane base with 6" #1606 chimney and #27 bobeche with six prisms (10.25" total). Crystal keyhole with 'Wildflower' plate etching on chimney: $500-550 pair; with ebony keyhole base: $550-650 pair. Gold encrusted items will command higher prices. (c. 1940-mid 1950s).

Cambridge close-up of 'Wildflower' etched chimney.

Cambridge 9.75" #1613 'Mt. Vernon' single light hurricane base with oversize bobeche and ten #7 (4") prisms. Crystal: $275-300 pair. Complete with 10" #1615 or 8" #1614 chimney: $400-450 pair. Hard to find. Possibly made in ruby and cobalt.

Far left:
Cambridge 'Caprice' coaster and **Heisey** 'Old Colony' mustard combined into a 13.5" electrified lamp. Crystal with gold: $100-125 each. (c. 1930s).

Left:
Cambridge-Heisey alternate view.

Cambridge 3.75" x 4.5" dolphin double light candle holder. Royal blue (cobalt): $750-800 pair; crystal: $350-400 pair; crown tuscan: $600-650 pair. All scarce.

Cambridge 5.625" x 5.5" #502 'Virginian' double light candle holder. Crystal: $135-150 pair. Also made as a candelabra. Shown in 1940 catalog.

Cambridge 6" x 8.625" #1580 epernette double light candle holder with 3.75" #1579 ball-shaped vase. Crystal: $200-225 pair. Shown in 1940 catalog.

Cambridge 9.5" #1474 'Lyre' double light candelabrum with #19 locking bobeches and #2 spearhead prisms. Crystal: $450-500 pair.

Cambridge alternate view.

Cambridge 11" x 11.25" #1442 'Lyre' double light candelabrum with #19 locking bobeches and #1 prisms (3"). Crystal: $700-750 pair. Also comes without bobeches or bobeche lips on candle cup. Compare to #1474; note different base and center finial.

Cambridge alternate view.

Cambridge 5.5" x 8" #1307 triple light candle holder. Crystal with #748 'Lorna' etching: $150-160 pair. (c. 1930s). Add 30% for colors.

Cambridge 6.125" #1307 triple light candle holder. Crown tuscan, royal blue: $300-325 pair; crystal: $100-115 pair; transparent pastels: $140-150 pair.

Below:
Cambridge 8" x 12.5" #1358/8 triple light candle base with #1438 'Cambridge Arms', two 8" vases, and #19 bobeches with #1 prisms. Crystal with alpine accents, crystal: $450-500 pair; moonlight blue with alpine, moonlight blue: $1000-1100 pair. (c. 1939-1945). This base is found with and without alpine accents.

Central Glass Works

Wheeling, West Virginia. **Central Glass Company** 1860s-1896; **Central Glass Works** 1896-1939. Tableware, bar goods, and stemware.

Central 3" #200 single light candle holder with gold-filled **Lotus** 'La Furiste' #0907 plate etching. Pink, green, amber, crystal: $65-70 pair. (c. 1920s).

Central 2.375" x 5.5" rolled edge single light candle holder. Pink with unknown silver floral overlay marked 'Sterling': $75-80 pair. Note: We have seen this silver overlay on some **Fostoria** pieces.

Central console set with 2.375" x 5.5" rolled edge single light candle holders and 13" rolled edge bowl. Pink with 'Sterling' overlay: $120-145 set.

Central 3.5" x 4.5" 'Old Spiral' single light candle holder with cutting. Green, pink, amber, crystal: $75-80 pair. (c. 1920s). Also comes in 8".

Central close-up of cutting.

Central 4.75" x 5" line #148 single light candle holder. Crystal with gold decoration and trim: $65-70 pair. This line was also used by **Seneca** for various cuttings and etchings. It was among **Central** assets purchased by **Imperial** in 1940.

Central line #148 console set with 4.75" single light candle holder and 12.5" bowl. Crystal with gold decoration and trim: $100-110 set.

Central 5.5" x 4.625" single light candle holder with cutting. Pink, green: $100-125 pair; crystal, amber: $80-85 pair. (c. 1920s). This blank was purchased and used by **Lotus**.

Central close-up of cutting.

Central 7" single light trumpet candle holder. Crystal with hand painted floral decoration and silver rings: $80-85 pair. (c. 1920s). Two-part mold.

Central 7" single light trumpet candle holder with cutting. Vaseline: $95-100 pair. (c. 1920s).

Central 8.375" x 4.75" 'Holly Motif' single light candle holder. Crystal with blue paint under base and gold decoration on a pressed band of 'Holly Motif' and on edges: $80-85 pair. Found with light blue, green, orange and possibly other colors under base; also found in crystal with gold trim on 'Holly Motif': $80-85 pair. (c. 1920s). Two-part mold.

Clarke "Pyramid" and "Fairy" Light Company

London, England, 1840s-1910. Other companies such as **Webb** made complete fairy light assemblies using Clarke patents for each of the separate pieces, while **Clarke** manufactured candles. Candles and candle lamps.

Clarke two-piece fairy lite. Dark blue/crystal: $225-250 each.

Clarke alternate view.

Consolidated Lamp & Glass Company

Beaver Falls, Pennsylvania, 1894-1933; 1936-1967 at Coraopolis, Pennsylvania. Illuminating wares, tableware, and occasional pieces.

Consolidated 3.75" #5640 'Beaded Edge' single light candle holders. White milk glass with 'Rose' hand decoration: $50-60 pair. (1950s). Initialed by decorator. Part of 'Con-Cora' line. Also found with 'Ivy' and 'Violet' hand decoration. An **Imperial** 'Candlewick' look-a-like.

Consolidated 'Beaded Edge' console set with 3.75" #5640 single light candle holders and #5636 5.125" x 10.75" footed fruit bowl. White milk glass with 'Rose' decoration and gold accents: $85-100 set.

Co-Operative Flint Glass Company

Beaver Falls, Pennsylvania. **Co-Operative Flint Glass Company Ltd.**, 1878-1889; **Co- Operative Flint Glass Company**, 1889-1937. Luncheon sets, giftware, and novelty items.

Co-Operative Flint 3" single light candle holder with floral and geometric cutting on base and edges. Ruby: $55-60 pair.

Co-Operative Flint 3.125" x 4.625" single light candle holder with gold encrusted plate etching. Green or other decorated colors: $65-70 pair; undecorated colors: $35-40 pair.

Co-Operative Flint close-up of plate etching.

Co-Operative Flint alternate view of plate etching.

Left:
Co-Operative Flint 3.125" single light candle holder. Crystal with orange painting under base and enameled flowers and gold trim: $55-60 pair. (c. 1920s).

Right:
Co-Operative Flint 9" #322 'Ray' or 'Douglass' single light candlestick. Crystal with amber stain cut-to-clear: $135-145 pair. (c. 1920s).

Bottom right:
Co-Operative Flint 9" close-up of cut-to-clear.

Co-Operative Flint 6.875" single light candle holder. Cobalt: $75-80 pair; black: $65-70 pair; canary: $70-75 pair. Also comes in 9". (c. 1920s).

Right:
Co-Operative Flint 7.25" #322 'Ray' or 'Douglass' single light candlestick. Blue: $120-130 pair; canary: $100-110 pair; midnight black, crystal: $75-80 pair; (possibly other colors). (c. 1920s). Will command higher prices with various cuttings or decorations.

Co-Operative Flint 9.25" and 7.5" #449 single light candle holders shown here for comparison of size. Blue, cobalt, green, amethyst: $130-140 pair; amber, crystal: $110-120 pair; sunset (c. 1925-1935): $175-185 pair. Part of #449 and #471 console sets.

Co-Operative Flint close-up of silver overlay.

Co-Operative Flint 9" #449 alternate view. Midnight black: $120-130 pair.

Co-Operative Flint 9.25" #449 alternate view. Sunset (introduced 1925): $175-185 pair. This same candle holder has been attributed to **Cambridge** (also from 1925) with the color listed as 'Tomato', but we can find no catalog documentation. Although **Cambridge** may have experimented with this color, this is a **Co-Operative Flint** form.

Co-Operative Flint 9" #449 alternate view. Ruby with heavy silver overlay: $200-225 pair. Three-part mold.

Czechoslovakia

Czechoslovakia 3.25" single light candle holder. Red orange with black glass trim: $100-110 pair.

Czechoslovakia 6.375" single light candle holder with blown stem and base and applied candle cup. Crystal with cranberry stain and gold trim: $140-150 pair.

Czechoslovakia (for Ralph Lauren) 5.25" single light candle holders. Dark red transparent: $35-40 pair.

Czechoslovakia (Prague) 6.75" four-sided candlestick with square base. Amber: $140-150 pair. (c. 1925-1935).

Czechoslovakia 7" single light candle/vase. Yellow/brown/orange mottled: $200-225 pair.

Czechoslovakia 7.875" single light candle holder. Dark brown amethyst with gold decoration on candle rim and base: $100-125 pair.

Czechoslovakia (Bohemian) 7.875" single light candle/vase. Marbled multicolor with rust and white: $250-275 pair.

Left:
Czechoslovakia 7" single light candle/vase. Amethyst with yellow glass spiral: $100-125 pair.

Right:
Czechoslovakia 8" single light candle holders. Crystal with orange lights, crystal with cobalt lights: $30-35 pair.

Czechoslovakia 8.5" single light candle holder with elongated bead stem. Dark amethyst: $110-125 pair.

Czechoslovakia 8.5" single light candle/vase. Crystal with yellow stain cut-to-clear: $300-350 pair.

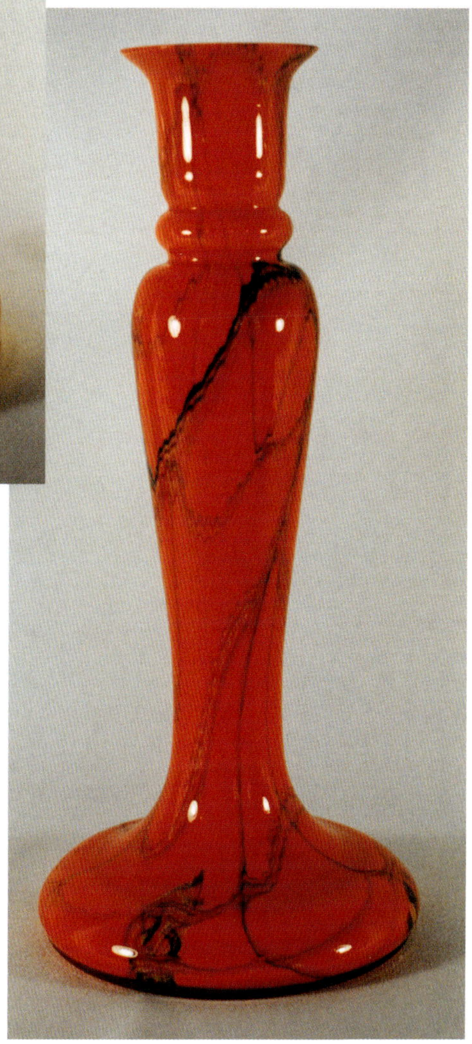

Left:
Czechoslovakia 8.5" single light candle holder. Crystal with cased orange candle cups and black column and base: $235-250 pair.

Right:
Czechoslovakia 8.625" single light candle holder. Crystal with cased orange and multicolored marble-like decoration: $300-350 pair.

Czechoslovakia 9.25" single light candle/vase. Red with black marbling: $300-350 pair.

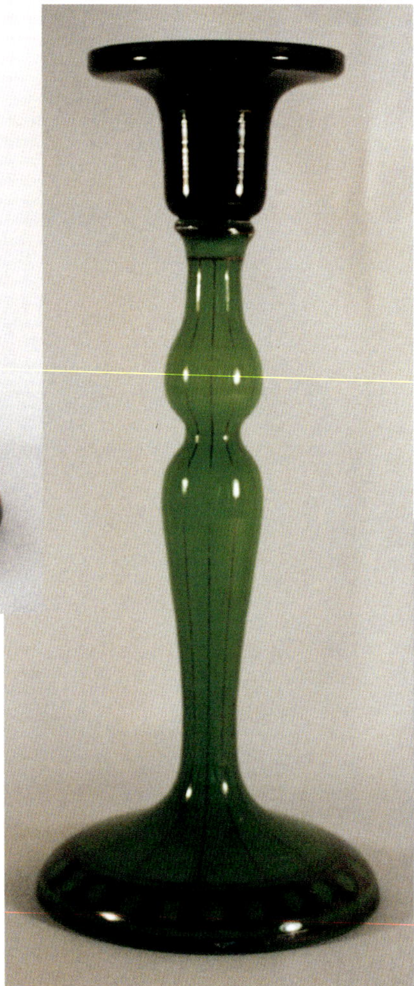

Czechoslovakia 9.375" single light candle holder. Green with silver decoration and black candle cup: $275-300 pair.

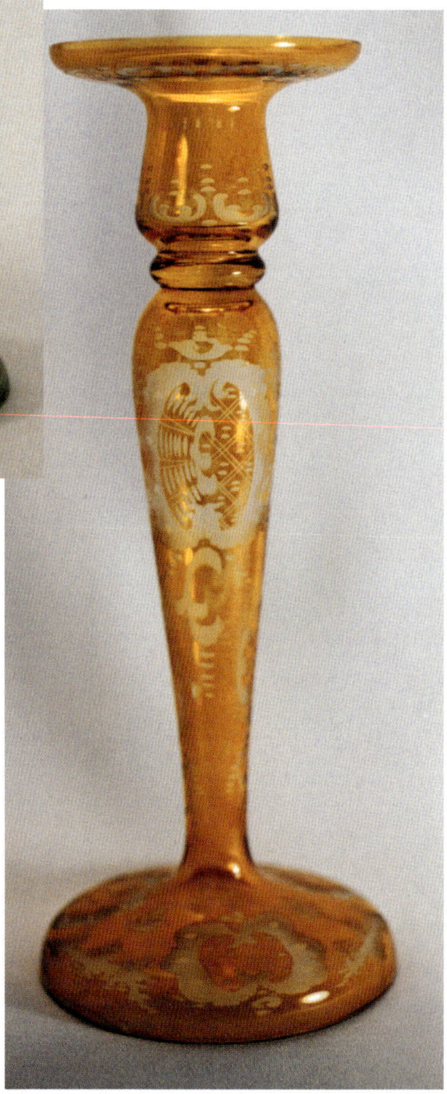

Czechoslovakia 10.25" single light candle holder. Crystal with amber stain and cut-to-clear: $350-400 pair.

Czechoslovakia alternate view of cut-to-clear.

Czechoslovakia alternate view.

Czechoslovakia (Bohemia) 10" single light lustre. Crystal with ruby stain cut-to-clear with stag and forest motif and large spearhead prisms: $1500-1600 pair. (c. 1890s). Notice cuttings on prisms.

Czechoslovakia alternate view.

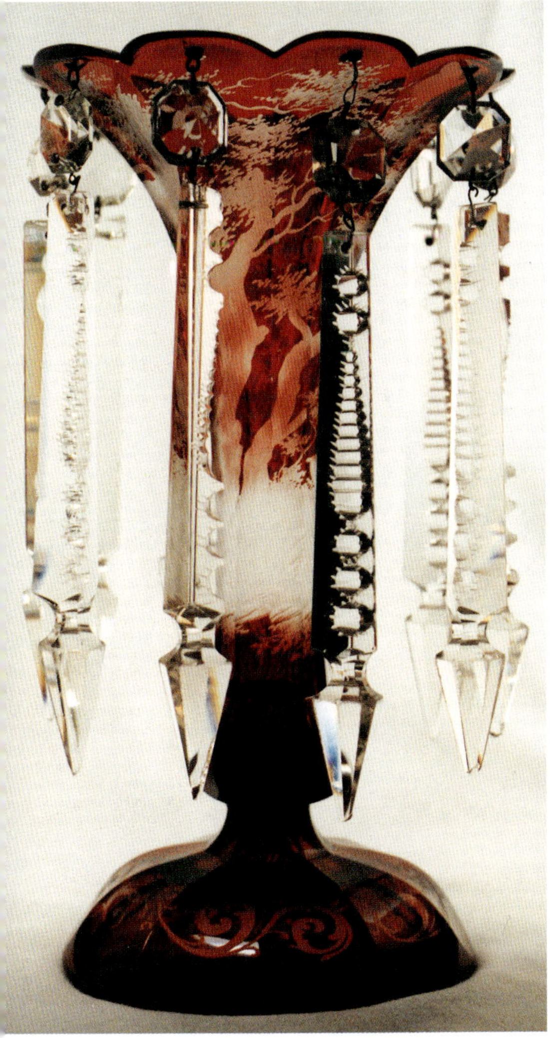

Czechoslovakia close-up of cut-to-clear.

Left:
Czechoslovakia 10.75" single light candle holder lustres. Ruby and opaque white cased glass cut-to-clear with large spearhead prisms: $950-1000 pair.

Right:
Czechoslovakia 11.25" single light lustres. Opaque blue with gold enameled stylized floral decoration and large spearhead prisms: $850-900 pair. (c. 1890s). Notice cuttings on prisms.

Czechoslovakia close-up of enamel.

Czechoslovakia 11.75" single light lustres. Ruby with enamel decoration and gold accents: $1250-1350 pair. (c. 1890s). Notice cuttings on the large prisms.

Czechoslovakia 13.25" single light lustres. Opaque white and pink cased glass with enameled periwinkle decoration and large spearhead prisms: $1250-1350 pair.

Czechoslovakia alternate view.

Czechoslovakia 13.5" single light candle holder lustre. Green and opaque white cased glass cut-to-clear with heavy gold geometric trim and large spearhead prisms: $950-1000 pair. Notice cuttings on prisms.

Czechoslovakia 'Art Deco' double light candle holder. Crystal: $135-150 pair. Paper label.

Czechoslovakia alternate view.

Czechoslovakia alternate view.

Czechoslovakia 6.5" triple light candle holder. Made in two pieces with the branched section applied to the hexagonal base. Crystal: $45-50 pair.

Czechoslovakia 9.75" triple light candle holder with cutting. Crystal: $100-125 pair. Fire polished.

Diamond Glassware Company

Indiana, Pennsylvania, 1916-1931. Tableware and occasional pieces.

Diamond 2.75" #713 single light candle holder. Green with black painted enamel background for enamel flowers gold trim: $45-50 pair.

Czechoslovakia 12.375" triple light candle holder made in two pieces with the branched section applied to the column. Crystal: $85-95 pair. Note the same candle branch used in both triple candle holders.

Right:
Diamond 7.125" single light blown candle/vase. Blue, green, cobalt: $70-75 pair; blue iridescent, green iridescent, marigold iridescent: $80-85 pair.

Diamond 9" single light trumpet candle holder. Green with heavy silver decoration: $75-85 pair. Notice the two rings under cup and the domed plunger.

Diamond 9.5" single light blown candle/vase. Green stretch, blue stretch, cobalt blue, marigold iridescent: $95-100 pair; blue satin: $75-80 pair. May be found with various decorations.

Duncan & Miller Glass Company

Washington, Pennsylvania, 1893-1955. Sold to **United States Glass Company** in 1955. The molds were transferred to Tiffin, Ohio. Dinnerware, tableware, and giftwares.

Duncan-Miller 1.75" x 5" #103 'Georgian' mushroom style single light candle holders. Amber, crystal: $40-45 pair; green, rose (pink): $45-50 pair. Fire polished.

Duncan-Miller 2.5" 'Triple Scroll' single light candle holder with **Lotus** 'La Furiste' #0907 plate etching. Crystal with gold encrusted trim, amber, green: $75-80 pair. Possibly made in pink.

Duncan-Miller close-up of 'La Furiste' plate etching.

Duncan-Miller 2.75" #125 'Murano' pattern #127 single light candle/flower arranger with 3.25" line #15 crimped violet vase and 5.25" line #15 crimped vase. Candle holder: blue opalescent, pink opalescent, crystal opalescent: $150-175 pair; crystal $60-65 pair; 3.25" vase: all opalescents: $30-35 each. 5.25" vase: all opalescents: $60-65 each. (c. 1930s-1950s).

Duncan-Miller 3.625" x 4.25" #50 three-paneled single light candle holder. Pink opalescent, blue opalescent: $110-125 pair; crystal opalescent: $95-100 pair.

Duncan-Miller 6.25" #16 'Art Deco' single light candle holder. Rose, green: $115-125 pair; crystal: $75-80 pair; ebony: $85-90 pair; cobalt, ruby: $140-150 pair. (c. 1920s-1930s). Will command a higher price with various etchings and decorations. **Lotus** used this candle holder for many of its lines.

Duncan-Miller 3.625" x 4.25" #50 three-paneled single light candle holder. Ruby, cobalt: $95-100 pair; crystal: $45-50 pair. Possibly made in rose, green, and amber.

Duncan-Miller 4" #118 'Hobnail' single light candle holders with 8" dessert plate. Crystal: $30-35 pair; rose, green, amber: $50-60 pair; white milk glass (#718-25): $55-60 pair; pink opalescent, blue opalescent, crystal opalescent: $60-65 pair. Dessert plate: $10-12 each.

George E. Duncan 8.385" 'Three Faces' mold single light candle holder; made in Portugal for Metropolitan Museum of Art. Crystal/crystal satin: $100-110 pair. Marked 'MMA'.

Duncan-Miller 7.5" #83 'Tavern' single light candle holder. Crystal with heavy cutting, crystal with decoration: $125-135 pair; crystal: $95-100 pair; crystal with iridized color: $110-120 pair. Also comes in 6" and 7.5".

Duncan-Miller 9.25" #40 'Spiral Flute' or 'Colonial Spiral' single light candle holder. Green, pink, amber: $165-175 pair; crystal: $95-100 pair; opalescent colors: $230-250 pair. Also comes in 7.5" and 11.5". *Reproduced* in very poor quality glass.

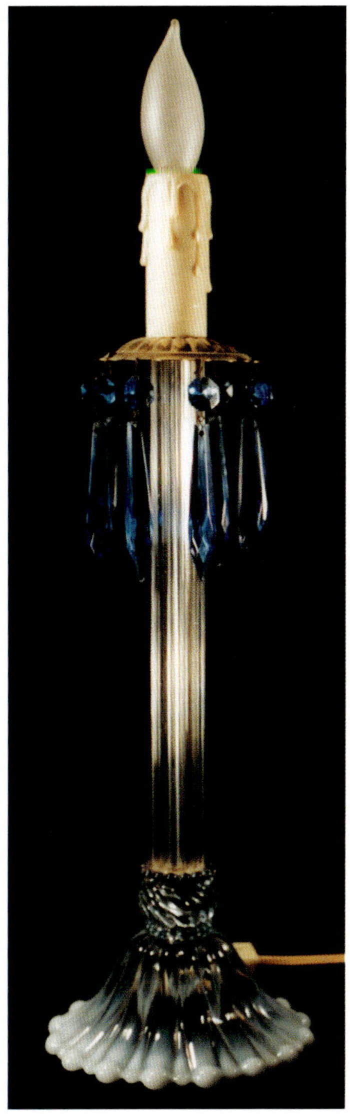

Duncan-Miller 4" (19.5" assembled) single light candle holder/lamp. Blue opalescent, pink opalescent: $260-275 pair.

Duncan-Miller 5.5" x 6.125" double light candle holder. Crystal: cannot price. We have not found documentation for this candle holder; however, it has the same stem and candle cups as line #115 'Canterbury', and it is beautiful glass. We feel this candle holder is a far better match with the line #115 low candle holder and the triple light candelabra than the one more often seen. Could this have been an earlier design that possibly did not sell well and was replaced with the double that is used now? We have placed this candle holder here in hopes of receiving information from our readers.

Duncan Miller 23.25" x 18.5" five-light 'Early American Sandwich' candelabrum with bobeches and prisms. Crystal only: $3250-3350 pair. **Note**: The three-light with a ball center is more difficult to find.

Durand Art Glass Company

Vineland, New Jersey, 1924-1931. Fine hand-blown art glass.

Durand 4.75" low mushroom style single light candle holders. Gold aurena: $1400-1500 pair. Signed. **Note**: Marked **Durand** pieces are difficult to find; the signature increases the value about 30%.

Durand alternate view showing signature.

England

England 5.125" single light candle holder. Crystal with pressed pattern and acid etched candle cup and birds: $40-45 pair.

England close-up of acid etched birds.

Durand console set with 4.75" candle holders and 13.75" bowl. Gold aurena: $2250-2500 set. All pieces signed.

England 5.5" six-sided single light candle holder. Vaseline: $90-100 pair.

England 7.875" single light candle holder. Vaseline: $115-125 pair.

England 8.5" single light candle holder with large base. Crystal with heavy cut multi-faceted stem and cup: $150-175 pair. (c. mid-late 1700s).

Fenton Art Glass Company

Williamstown, West Virginia, 1906 to present. Iridescent or "Carnival" glassware, art glass, and giftware.

Fenton 1.375" x 4.375" #848 three-footed single light candle bowl. Jade (c. 1933-1936): $50-55 pair; crystal: $15-20 pair; black (c. 1933): $35-40 pair; ruby (c. 1933-1936): $45-50 pair; moonstone (c. 1933): $55-60 pair; Chinese yellow (c. 1933), royal blue (1933-1936), green transparent (1935): $65-70 pair.

Fenton table center with 2.125" x 5" #1091'Basket Weave with Open Edge' three-footed candle bowls and 7" bowl. Candle holders: light green (1935): $50-55 pair; black: $35-40 pair; jade, green opalescent, ruby (1936): $60-65 pair. Set: $90-100.

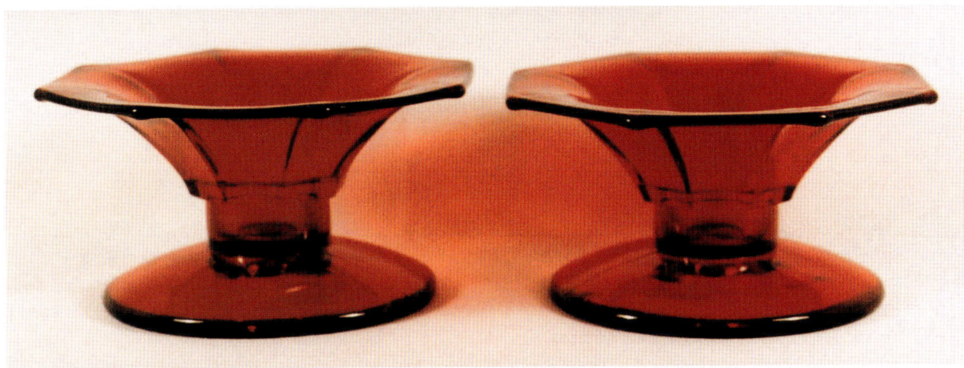

Fenton 2.62" x 5" #1672 eight-paneled flared single light candle holder with round base (also came with rolled edge). Ruby (1933): $75-80 pair; black (1933): $45-50 pair; jade green (1931): $70-75 pair; lilac (1933): $150-160 pair.

Fenton 2.625" #318 single light candle holder. Jade (c. 1933), ruby (1933), cameo opalescent (1926), aquamarine (c. 1928): $70-80 pair; black (c. 1933): $50-55 pair; rose (1928), light green: $50-60 pair; Chinese yellow: $70-75 pair; Pekin blue (c. 1933): $100-110 pair; Mandarin red: $120-130 pair.

Fenton 3.25" #315 'Princess' single light saucer candle holder. Ruby, jade: $80-85 pair; topaz stretch, Florentine green stretch, Chinese yellow: $90-95 pair; Celeste blue stretch: $130-140 pair; wisteria stretch: $160-170 pair.

Fenton 2.625" #318 single light candle holder. Mandarin red: $120-130 pair.

Fenton 3.375" #316 single light candle holder. Jade (1931): $75-80 pair; black, rose (1928): $60-65 pair; cameo opalescent (c. 1926): $80-85 pair; ruby (1933): $80-85 pair.

Fenton 3.5" #316 single light candle holder. Stretch glass: velva rose, topaz, celeste blue: $100-110 pair; Florentine green, Persian pearl: $90-95 pair; tangerine: $130-140 pair. (c. 1920s).

Fenton 3.5" #1623 'Dolphin' single light candle holders. Rose, green, gold: $90-95 pair; ruby: $120-130 pair; crystal with satin: $70-75 pair; tangerine, orchid: $100-110 pair. (c. 1927-1932).

Fenton 3.625" #1800 'Sheffield' single light candle holder with silver floral overlay and rings. Crystal: $40-45 pair; crystal with 'Silverton' etching: $60-65 pair; crystal with 'Ming' etching, gold with 'Silverton' etching: $70-75 pair; blue with 'Silverton' etching: $90-95 pair. (c. 1936-1938). Reissued in 1986 as #6672 'New Sheffield' in peaches and cream opalescent: $70-75 pair.

Fenton 4.5" #5204AY 'Atlantis' two-piece fish fairy lite with three panels. Red carnival: $60-65 each. (c. 2001). Signed '2001Thomas K. Fenton #957'. Limited edition.

Fenton 3.875" #8475 'Lily-of-the-Valley' single light candle holder. Cameo opalescent, blue opalescent, pink opalescent (champagne satin): $70-75 pair; topaz opalescent: $90-95 pair. (c. 1979-1982).

Fenton 4.5" #5405TK 'Lily Trail' two-piece fairy lite with hand painted dragonfly and floral decoration. Topaz iridescent, light yellow iridescent: $50-55 each. (c. 2001). Signed. Limited edition.

Right:
Fenton 4.625" #5204AY 'Atlantis' two-piece fish fairy lite with three panels. Light green iridescent: $50-55 each. (c. 2001).

Below:
Fenton 4.5" #5204AY 'Atlantis' two-piece fish fairy lites with three panels. Violet: $50-55 each.

Fenton 4.75" #7300GV 'Lenton Rose' two-piece fairy lite. Golden glow: $60-65 each. (c. 1999). Limited edition.

Fenton 4.75" #300MJ 'Vermont Sky' two-piece fairy lite. Spruce green with log cabin country scene: $60-65 each. (c. 2000). Signed 'S. Smith'. Limited edition.

Fenton 4.75" #7300LB 'Winter Memories' two-piece fairy lite. Gold iridescent: $55-60 each. (c. 2000). Limited edition.

Fenton 4.75" #7300KY 'Butterfly Garden' two-piece fairy lite. Cobalt with crystal base: $45-50 each. (c. 2000). Limited edition.

Fenton 4.75" #7300 'The Arrival' limited edition of 'Birth of Savior' fairy lite series: $70-75 each. (c. 2000).

Fenton 4.75" #7300 'Woodland Frost' two-piece fairy lite. French opalescent iridized satin with snow and evergreen trees: $60-65 each. (c. 2000). Limited edition.

Fenton 5.625" x 4.375" #8405YH 'Spring Splendor' two-piece fairy lite. Pink chiffon iridescent with hand painted floral decoration and pressed floral and bead pattern: $50-55 each. (c. 2001). Signed.

Fenton 5.125" #9407CP two-piece fairy lite with strawberries. Pink iridescent: $30-35 each. (c. 1999).

Fenton 5.625" x 4.375" #8405WQ 'Whispering Winds' two-piece fairy lite. Willow green: $50-55 each. (c. 2000).

Fenton 4.625" #1523 or #7270 single light candle holder. Aqua crest (1942-1943), emerald crest (1950-1952): $140-150 pair; silver crest (1943-1954), gold crest (1943-1944): $75-80 pair; ivory crest (1940-1942): $90-95 pair; crystal crest (1942), peach crest (1940-1954), rose crest (1946-1948): $120-130 pair; Blue Ridge (1939-1940): $150-160 pair.

Fenton 7" x 4.5" #8404L9 'Lily-of-the-Valley' two-piece fairy lite. Ice blue pearl (blue iridescent) with pressed pattern: $45-50 each. (c. 2001).

Fenton 5.375" #6 'Swan' single light candle holder. Crystal/crystal satin, crystal, crystal satin: $150-160 pair; milk glass: $170-180 pair. (c. 1938). There are varying opinions whether the rare blue opalescent candle holder, valued at $450-500 pair, is Fenton's.

Fenton alternate view.

Fenton 5.75" #950 cornucopia single light candle holder/vase. Jade: $100-110 pair. (c. 1932).

Fenton 5.75" #950 cornucopia single light candle holder/vase. Royal blue (cobalt): $130-140 pair. (c.1934).

Fenton 6" #951 "Aqua Crest' cornucopia single light candle holder/vase. White with aqua rim: $110-120 pair. (c. 1941-1943).

Fenton 6" #950 cornucopia single light candle holder/vase on fitted metal filigree base. Crystal with crystal satin 'San Toy' etched pattern: $140-150 pair. (c. 1936).

Fenton close-up of applied filigree base.

Fenton 6" #6370 'Flower Band' single light candle holder. Forget me not blue: $40-45 pair. Introduced in 1982.

Fenton 7" x 5.5" #6190 (old **Westmoreland** #1710/8 'Wagner' mold) swirl single light candle holder. Ruby: $70-75 pair. (c. 1999). Marked with a cursive 'F' inside an oval; this mark was introduced in 1983 to indicate molds purchased from other companies.

Fenton close-up of 'Flower Band' pattern.

Fenton #3472 three-piece table center with 11.5" #3778 candle bowl, 7" #3745 candle holder, and #3746 candle epergne. White milk glass: $150-165 set. (c. 1973-1976).

Fenton 11" #3998MI 'Hobnail' hurricane lamp. White milk glass: $60-65 each (1952-1970); blue pastel: $150-160 each (1954-1955); green pastel: $125-135 each (1954-1956); rose pastel: $100-110 each (1954-1955).

Fenton alternate view.

Fenton 8.25" #3998 single light hurricane lamp. Peach Blow (cased glass with gold ruby interior and milk glass exterior): $130-140 each. (c. 1952-1954).

Fenton 9.5" #389 'Moonstone' single light hurricane lamp. Base with hand decorated globe: $45-50 each. We cannot verify that the globe is **Fenton**.

Fenton 8.75" #1167OQ 'Hobnail' three-piece fairy lite. Violet iridescent with cream opalescent cup: $90-95 each. (c. 2001).

Fenton alternate view.

Fenton alternate view.

Fenton 8.25" #549 single light candle holder. Florentine green stretch: $175-185 pair; celeste blue stretch, Grecian gold iridescent: $200-215 pair; Persian pearl stretch: $260-275 pair. ;(c. 1922-1928). Also found in opaques and many combinations of opaque and stretch.

Fenton 8.25" #9071 'Colonial' single light candlestick. Ivory (almond) satin with hand painted decoration: $95-100 pair (c. 2000). Signed. Paper '95' label. Also available in black with various decorations (1990s).

Fenton 8.5" #9071 'Colonial' single light candle holder. Ivory (almond) satin with rust-pink Christmas floral decoration (1999), 'Twining Berries' decoration (1998): $100-110 pair.

Fenton 8.375" #9071 'Colonial' single light candle holder. Petal pink, twilight blue: $65-70 pair; sea mist green: $70-75 pair. (c. 1992-1996), sea green satin (pearlized) (1998): $60-65 pair.

Fenton 8.625" #9071 'Colonial' single light candle holder. Crystal with deep cut floral decoration: $80-85 pair. (c. 1920s). Note the deeper base.

Fenton 10.25" #7520QP "The Journey" limited edition hurricane lamp. Spruce satin: $170-180 each. (c. 2000).

Fenton 10" #349 single light candle holder with 'Oval Cut' pattern. Celeste blue: $275-300 pair. The candle rim has been cut off and polished so that this candle holder can be used as a lamp base. (c. 1923).

Fenton close-up of cutting.

Fenton 10.685" #349 single light candle holder. Ruby stretch (scarce): $550-600 pair; wisteria: $300-325 pair; Florentine green: $350-375 pair; Persian pearl, velva rose, topaz: $375-400 pair. (c. 1920s). **Note**: The darker and more even the iridescence, the greater the value.

Fenton 12" #349 and 8" #449 single light candle holders shown here for comparison. Grecian gold: 12": $375-400 pair; 8": $265-280 pair.

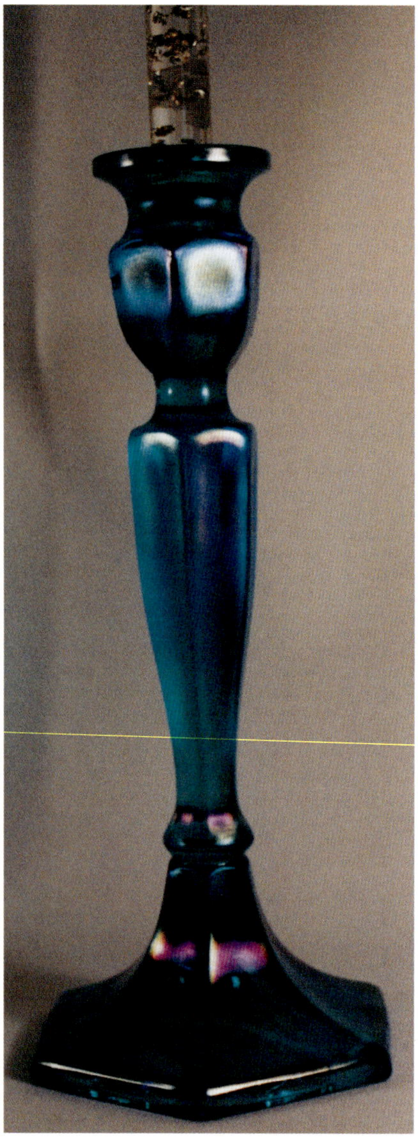

Fenton 10.5" #349 'Colonial' single light candle holder. Celeste blue iridescent: $375-400 pair. Two-part mold.

Right:
Fenton 11.75" #8376 'Valencia' hurricane lamp with custom-sized crystal globe. Dusty rose, Provencal blue opalescent: $30-35 each; teal royale, colonial amber: $25-30 each; rose corsage (pearlized pink): $40-45 each; white satin with 'Holly Berry' decoration: $50-55 each. (1980s).

Vineland 10.125" 'Colonial' single light candle holder shown here for comparison. Russet stretch, pink stretch, old gold, wisteria iridescent, Tut blue iridescent: $275-325 pair. Three-part mold. **Fenton** sticks are two-part molds.

Fenton 15" #9471 single light hurricane lamp. Spruce green, ruby: $50-55 each. (c. 2000).

Fenton 5.75" x 5.25" #2000 'Pineapple' double light candle holder. Blue-grey: cannot price. This color is not listed for this pattern in any of our references; however we feel that this is the rare color 'Mermaid Blue' (c. 1938). It is a beautiful grey-blue or steel-blue, and it fits the time frame during which the color was made. Colors listed for 'Pineapple': crystal satin: $160-170 pair; rose satin: $190-210 pair; ruby: $350-400 pair; royal blue: $420-460 pair.

Fenton 7.625" x 18.5"'Hobnail' centerpiece. White milk glass wedding bowl with ribbon edges on brass with white milk glass base and lights: $125-150 each. Probably purchased and assembled by another company.

Fenton 6.75" x 14.75" wedding bowl centerpiece. Cranberry opalescent on brass with milk glass base and lights: $225-250 each. Probably purchased and assembled by another company.

Fostoria Glass Company

Moundsville, West Virginia, 1887-1983. Purchased by **Lancaster Glass.** Dinnerware, pressed ware, and gift items.

Fostoria 1.75" x 4.5" #2394 single light footed candle bowl with #291 'Palm Leaf' brocade etching and decoration #73 Mother of Pearl iridescence and gold trim. Rose, green: $170-180 pair. (c. 1929).

Fostoria close-up of 'Palm Leaf' brocade decoration.

Fostoria 1.75" x 4.5" #2394 three-footed single light candle bowl upside down to show #290 'Oak Leaf' brocade etching. Green, rose: $140-150 pair; crystal $130-140 pair. (c. 1928-1930).

Fostoria 3" x 4.5" #2324 'Coronada' decoration #49 single light candle holder. Blue with dark band of paint under base and gold encrusted plate etching #273 'Royal' on top of base plus gold rings: $80-85 pair. (c. 1925-1927). 'Royal' was **Fostoria's** first complete table service etched in crystal and colors.

Fostoria 3.25" #2324 single light candle holder. Crystal with unknown silver encrusted plate etching and silver rings: $60-65 pair. (c. 1925-1982).

Fostoria 2.25" # 2324 low single light candle holder with cutting on bottom of base. Blue, orchid, azure: $60-65 pair; ebony, amber, crystal: $40-45 pair; rose, green; $50-55 pair. (c. 1925-1940).

Fostoria close-up of etching.

Fostoria 3.375" #2324 single light candle holder. Crystal with unknown cutting: $50-55 pair. (c. 1925-1982).

Fostoria close-up of cutting.

Fostoria 3.25" #2324 single light candle holder. Amber with unidentified etching with gold encrusted birds: $70-75 pair. (c. 1925-1940).

Fostoria 3.25" x 4.5" #2395 'Double Scroll' single light candle holder with #287 'Versailles' etching. Green, rose, topaz: $80-85 pair; azure: $115-125 pair. (c. 1928-1924).

Fostoria close-up of 'Versailles' etching.

Fostoria 3" #2375 'Fairfax' single light candle holder with #278 'Versailles' etching. Rose, topaz, green: $70-75 pair; azure: $80-85 pair. (c. 1928-1939).

Fostoria close-up of 'Versailles' etching. Note variations in the etching.

Fostoria 'Fairfax' alternate view showing 'Oakwood' decoration #72 or 'Oak Leaf' #290 brocade plate etching with decoration #72 Mother of Pearl iridescence and gold trim. Orchid, azure: $150-160 pair. (c. 1928-1929).

Fostoria 3.75" #2560 ° 'Coronet' single light candle holder with #333 'Willomere' etching. Crystal only: $50-55 pair. (c. 1938-1957).

Fostoria close-up of etching.

Fostoria alternate view of #2560 ° 'Coronet' showing #785 'Cynthia' cutting on base. Crystal only: $50-55 pair. (c. 1938-1957). Do not confuse with #170 'Cynthia'.

Fostoria 5" #2395 ° 'Double Scroll' single light candle holder with #279 'June' etching. Topaz: $100-110 pair; crystal: $80-95 pair; rose, azure: $150-160 pair. (c. 1930-1939).

Fostoria 5.375" #2470 ° four-footed candle holder with #316 'Midnight Rose' plate etching. Crystal only: $130-140 pair. (c. 1933-1945). Compare with the #333 'Willomere' etching.

Fostoria 5.5" #2535 single light candle holder. Ruby, regal blue (cobalt), burgundy, empire green: $140-150 pair; crystal: $90-95 pair. (c. 1935-1940).

Left:
Fostoria 5.625" #2470 single light candle holder with #313 'Morning Glory' plate etching. Crystal: $130-140 pair; crystal with amber base: $160-170 pair. (c. 1933-1934).

Below:
Fostoria close-up of 'Morning Glory' plate etching.

Fostoria 5.375" #2470 ° single light candle holder. Green, rose, topaz: $90-100 pair; crystal: $60-65 pair; amber: $80-85 pair; wisteria: $140-150 pair; ruby: $160-170 pair; regal blue (cobalt), burgundy, empire green: $200-220 pair. (c. 1933-1945).

Left:
Fostoria 5.625" #2470 single light candle holder with #309 'Legion' plate etching on bowl. Rose/crystal: $170-180 pair; all crystal: $140-150 pair; topaz/crystal: $150-160 pair. (c. 1933-1934).

Right:
Fostoria 6.125" #2269 'Art Deco' single light candle holder. Green: $120-130 pair; crystal: $100-110 pair; amber, ebony: $110-120 pair; blue: $130-140 pair; canary: $140-150 pair. Can be found with deep etchings and various decorations. (c. 1920s).

Fostoria 6.375" #2675 'Randolph' single light candle holders and 8.5" #1200/792 celery vase. White milk glass (c. 1955-1965): $55-60 pair; peach milk glass, aqua milk glass (both c. 1957-1959): $70-75 pair. Vase (1957-1965): $35-40 each.

Left:
Fostoria 7" #2297 'Modern' single light candlestick. Amber with cutting, ebony: $110-120 pair; blue, green: $120-130 pair. (c. 1924-1927).

Right:
Fostoria 6.875" #2297 'Modern' single light candle holder. Canary with cutting: $150-160 pair. (c. 1924-1926).

Far left:
Fostoria 6.75" #2482 (altered) single light candle holder with #318 'Springtime' plate etching. Crystal: $80-85 pair. (c. 1934-1933). **Note**: This candle holder does not appear in Fostoria catalogs. We believe it was made by removing the arms from a broken #2482 trindle candle holder and fire polishing the cuts. It makes a pretty candle holder.

Left:
Fostoria close-up of etching.

Fostoria 7.5" #2545 'Flame' single light candle holder lustres with prisms. Crystal: $135-145 pair; gold tint: $150-160 pair; azure: $160-170 pair. (c. 1936-1942).

Fostoria 7.5" #2453 single light lustre with eight prisms. Crystal (c. 1933-1940; 1953-1957): $160-170 pair; ebony (c. 1953-1957), green (c. 1933-1934): $200-220 pair; amber (c. 1933-1934): $180-190 pair; topaz (c. 1933-1934): $190-200 pair; wisteria (c. 1933-1934): $270-290 pair.

Fostoria 7.75" #1218 single light square candlestick. Crystal with floral etching: $150-160 pair. (c. 1920s).

Left:
Fostoria 8" #1485 single light candlestick. Crystal with deep etched floral pattern and solid hexagonal base. Crystal: $150-160 pair. (c. 1920s). Also comes in 11".

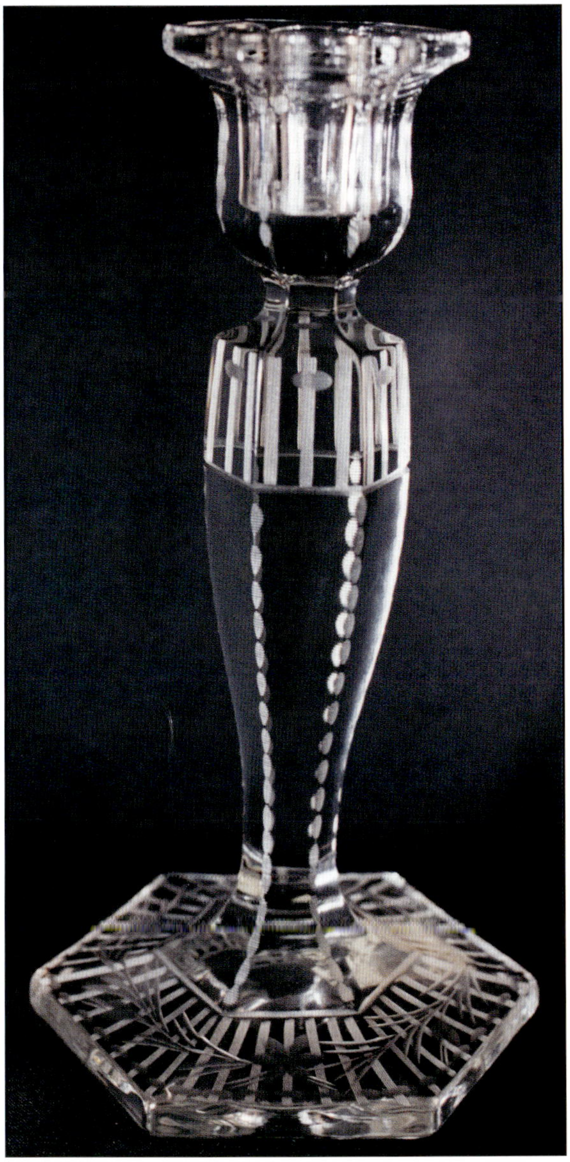

Left:
Fostoria 8" #1485 single light candle holder. Crystal with cutting on candle cup and column with floral cutting on base: $150-160 pair. (c. 1920s).

Right:
Fostoria 8.25" #2436 single light lustre. Crystal (c. 1930-1940): $120-130 pair; amber: $130-140 pair; green, topaz, ebony: $150-160 pair; rose: $180-190 pair; wisteria: $200-220 pair. (Colors c. 1930-1934).

Fostoria close-up of etching.

Fostoria 8.25" #2245 single light candle holder. Canary, blue: $100-110 pair; crystal, amber: $130-140 pair; green, ebony: $150-160 pair. (c. 1909-1928). Also found deep etched and with various decorations.

Far left:
Fostoria 8.375" #1965 single light candlestick with four-sided, three-step base. Crystal with deep 'Roman' etching: $170-180 pair. (c. 1920s).

Left:
Fostoria close-up of etching.

Fostoria 9" #2324 single light candlestick with #273 'Royal' etching. Amber: $80-85 pair; crystal: $60-65 pair; green: $90-95 pair; blue: $100-110 pair. (c. 1925-1927). Also comes in 2", 4" and 12".

Fostoria 9" #2324 single light candlestick. Crystal with deep etching: $80-85 pair. (c. 1925-1929).

Fostoria 9" 'Grape Stem' single light candle holder. Amber with heavy gold decoration: $275-300 pair. (c. 1920s). This column was also used for the #2325 small boudoir lamp.

Fostoria 9.5" #4 'Colony' line #2412 single light lustre candle holder with ten 'U' prisms. Crystal: $200-220 pair. (c. 1889-1909; 1934-1940).

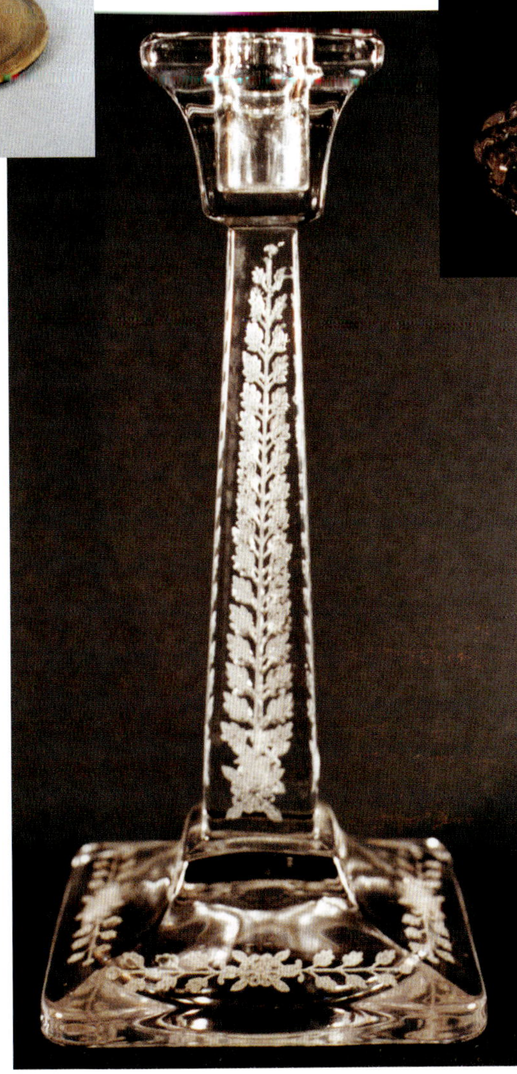

Fostoria 9.25" #1964 single light candlestick with square column. Crystal with deep etching: $190-200 pair. (c. 1920-1925).

Fostoria 15.25" #19 single light candle pillar. Crystal: $250-265 pair; with cutting: $285-300 pair. (c. 1890-1916). Also comes in 7" (1935), 10", 12", and 18".

Fostoria 11.875" #19 single light candle pillar. Wisteria: cannot price. We have not found this color listed, but believe it may have resulted from exposure to the sun.

Fostoria 3.375" x 13.25" #2415 'Combination Bowl' double light candle bowl with elaborate floral cutting. Topaz: $245-265 each.

Left:
Fostoria 3.375" x 13.25" #2415 'Combination Bowl' double light candle bowl with mercury glass candles. Ebony, green, rose, topaz: $60-65 each; azure: $65-70 each. (c. 1929).

Center Left:
Fostoria 5.125" x 6.5" #2447 double light candle holder. Wisteria: $150-160 pair; topaz, ebony, amber: $85-90 pair; crystal: $75-80 pair; green, rose: $95-100 pair; azure: $100-110 pair. (c. 1931-1939).

Below:
Fostoria 5.25" x 6.5" #2447 double light candle holder. Topaz: $85-90 pair.

Fostoria close-up of cutting.

Fostoria 8.125" x 8" #2484 'Baroque' double light candle holders. Silver mist, crystal: $75-80 pair; topaz (gold tint): $110-120 pair; azure: $120-130 pair. (Silver mist: c. 1935-1938; others: c. 1935-1965).

Fostoria console set with 8.125" #2484 double light candle holders and 3.125" x 12.25" elongated octagonal bowl with leaf pattern. Silver mist: $115-125 set.

Fostoria 4.25" x 7.75" #2383 triple light candle holder. Green, rose, azure: $120-130 pair; crystal: $100-110 pair; amber, topaz, ebony: $110-120 pair. (c. 1928-1939).

France

Portieux and **Vallerysthall,** both having originated in the 1700s, merged in 1872 to become **Vallerysthall et Portieux**. They separated in the mid 1950s and **Portieux** closed in the mid-1980s. **Vallerysthall** is still in production, but on a small scale.

France 2.375" x 3.5" #62510 single light candle holder. Red violet: $20-25 pair.

France 2.5" x 8" single light candle holder with glass flowers. Green/pink: $35-40 pair.

France (Baccarat) 3.25" three-footed single light candle holder. Crystal: $200-250 pair.

Left:
France (Baccarat) 8" single light candlestick. Crystal: $300-325 pair.

Below:
France (Baccarat) 9.375" #928.030 'Segur' single light lamp standard. Crystal: $500-550 each. Also came with prisms. Mold marked.

France (Portieux) 7.875" 'Chimeres' single light candle holder. This candle holder is very ornate with mythical winged reptilian birds. Blue milk glass, white milk glass: $160-175 pair. (c. 1930s). Hard to find.

France close-up of pattern on column.

France 8" single light candlestick. Amber: $275-300 pair.

France (Portieux) 9.875" single light candlestick. This candle holder is very elegant with a swirled column. Blue: $300-325 pair. May come in other colors.

France (Vallerysthall) 9.125" single light candle holder. This candle holder is very ornate with fruit, leaves and vines; the base has beaded circles. Green: $200-250 pair; may come in other colors. Marked.

France 10.375" single light hunter figural candlestick. Crystal satin, white milk glass: $325-350 pair.

France alternate views.

France 9.5" single light candle holder with three dolphin feet. Blue milk glass: $200-250 pair.

France close-up of dolphins.

France 9.5" single light candle holder with three dolphin feet. White opal, blue milk glass: $200-250 pair. *Reproduced* in transparent colors in poor quality glass.

France 8" x 6.5" double light candle holder. Crystal: $200-225 pair. This is made from a very heavy glass cylinder twisted back on itself. Marked diamond 'ART Vincinne France' (acid etched).

H.C. Fry Glass Company

Rochester Pennsylvania, 1901-1929. Continued production in receivership from 1929-1933. Purchased by Libbey Glass in 1933. Cut glass, colorful art glass, and "Pearl Glass" opalescent colored bakeware.

Left:
Fry 4.125" single light candle holder with crystal swirl ball stem connector. Amethyst, royal blue: $135-145 pair; black, emerald: $125-135 pair. Note the drip plate and the scalloped base.

Right:
Fry 8" single light candle holder with 'Daisy' cutting. Crystal: $800-850 pair.

Germany & West Germany

Germany 3.875" single light footed candle vase. Crystal with red stain: $70-75 pair; crystal: $55-60 pair.

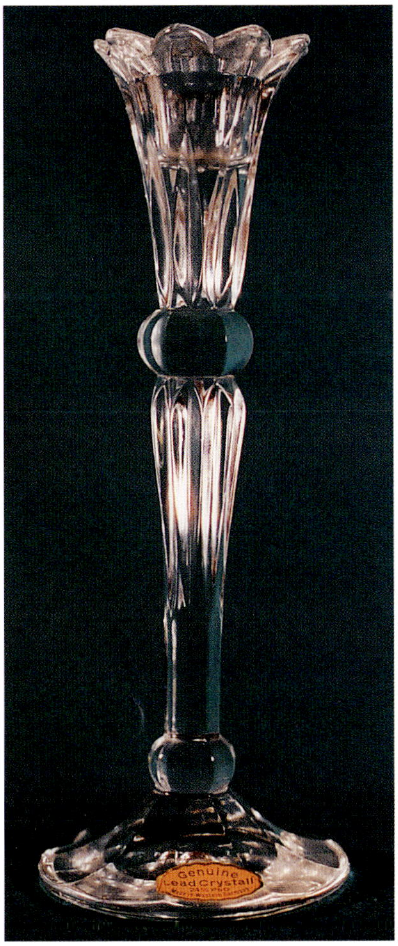

Left:
West Germany 8" single light candlestick. Lead crystal (24%): $55-60 pair. Paper label.

Right:
West Germany 10" single light 24% lead crystal candlestick. Royal blue: $70-75 pair.

Below right:
West Germany 10.5" single light lustre candle holder. White with heavy gold floral decoration and large spearhead prisms: $650-700 pair. Paper label. Notice cuttings on prisms. These were also used for lamps.

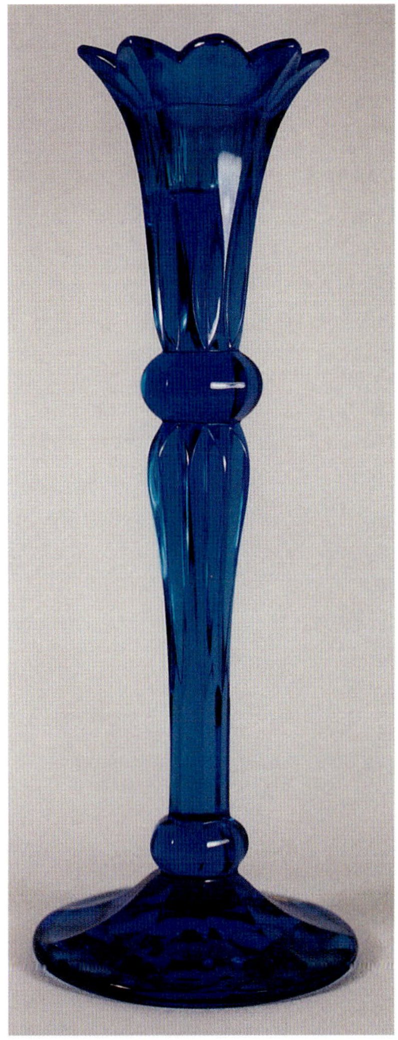

Germany (Rosenthal) close-up of 'Classic Rose' pattern.

Left:
Germany (Rosenthal) 6.125" 'Classic Rose' single light candle holder. Crystal with enameled white/blue/gold decoration: $70-75 pair. Marked.

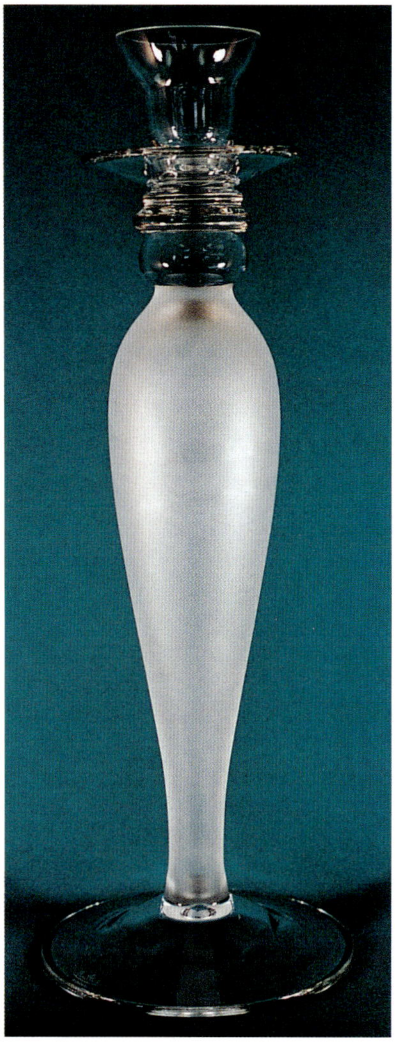

Germany (Rosenthal) 16.5" single light candlestick. Crystal/crystal satin: $200-225 pair. Marked 'Rosenthal Classic'.

Germany (Rosenthal) 16.5" single light candlestick. Crystal/cobalt satin: $225-250 pair. Marked 'Rosenthal Classic'.

Germany 4" double light candle holder. Crystal with red stain: $70-75 pair; crystal, crystal satin: $55-60 pair.

West Germany 6.5" x 7.25" triple light candelabra. Lead crystal (24%): $95-100 pair. This candelabra has three separate branches joined at the column.

Hawkes Rich Cut-Glass Co.

Corning, New York, 1880-1962. Later **T.G. Hawkes & Co**. Beautiful occasional pieces, tableware, and stemware.

Hawkes alternate view with modified **Fostoria** candle insert at side.

Hawkes (**Heisey** #100 'Centennial' blank) 6" single light candlestick. Crystal with floral cutting on light and base: $200-225 pair.

Hawkes alternate view.

Hawkes close-up of floral cutting.

Hawkes 3.25" x 6.75" single light candle bowl with duck engraving. Ruby stain cut-to-clear: $450-500 each. (early 1970s). We believe this candle holder was cut for **Hawkes Crystal**, probably by Floyd Manwarren.

Hawkes 6" (**Heisey** #100 'Centennial' blank) single light candle holders. Crystal with yellow stain cut-to-clear and gold trim: $300-350 pair. Signed.

Hawkes 6" (**Heisey** #100 'Centennial' blank) single light candle holder. Crystal with cutting: $200-225 pair.

Hawkes console with 6" single light candle holders and 8" bowl: $450-500 set. Signed.

Hawkes 12" single light candlestick. Crystal with bird and floral cutting, fretting on the light and cutting on top of the light. $900-1000 pair

Hawkes alternate view.

Hawkes close-ups of bird cutting.

A.H. Heisey & Company

Newark, Ohio, 1896-1958. Some molds were purchased by **Imperial Glass Company**. Elegant stemware and tableware.

Heisey 1.5" x 7.25" #1540 'Lariat' single light hurricane base with handle. Crystal with 'Charleton' hand painted floral decoration: $95-100 pair; complete with #5040 chimney: $500-550 pair. (c. 1942-1950). Found with and without handle. Few marked. **Note**: 'Charleton' was a registered trademark for hand decorations done by Abels, Wasserberg & Co., Inc. of New York.

Heisey 1.75" #1205 'Raindrop' single light candle holders. Flamingo: $95-100 pair; moongleam: $110-120 pair; crystal: $55-60 pair; gold opalescent (marigold/gold with opalescent edge): $850-900 pair (experimental color; very scarce). (c. 1929). Usually marked.

Heisey 2" #1503-1/2 'Crystolite' single light melon candle blocks with bottoms ground and polished. Crystal only: $50-60 pair. (c. 1941-1945). Not marked. This candle block was not reissued and therefore is less common than other 1503 blocks. **Note**: If you find one with a hole cut all the way through, this is a lamp part used in later years.

Heisey 4.75" x 5" #1469 'Ridgeleigh' single light candle vase. Zircon: $365-395 pair; sahara: $175-185 pair; crystal: $75-80 pair. (c. 1936-1940). Some marked.

Heisey console set with 5" candle holders and 3.25" x 11" bowl: $675-725 set.

Below:
Heisey 18.5" 'Ridgeleigh' electrified lamp with 3" coaster base, 2.5" coaster on top and two metal wafers. Vase: $35-40. Coasters: $20-25 each. Lamp: $100-125 each. (c. 1936-1940). An unmodified candle vase is included for comparison.

Below right:
Heisey alternate view.

Heisey 3.5" #1533 'Wampum' candle holder in 2" x 13.5" gardenia bowl. Crystal. Candle holders: $85-90 pair; bowl: $90-95 each. (c. 1941-1942). Some marked.

Heisey 8.75" 'Wampum' candle holder and #5 epergne (peg insert vase) in 2" x 13.5" gardenia bowl. Crystal: $200-225 three-piece set.

Left:
Heisey 5.625" (5") #16 'Classic' single light candle holder. Crystal only: $140-150 pair. (c. 1906-1931). Some marked. Also comes in 7", 9", and 11". This candle holder was used as the base for several candelabra and electro-portable lamps.

Opposite page, bottom left:
Heisey 7.5" #47 'Regal' four-sided single light candlestick with bulbous column. Crystal with #336 'Rosette Band' plate etching. Crystal only: $250-275 pair. (1912-1929; etching introduced in 1916). Some marked. This candle holder has been cut on top and has a puntied (polished to a depressed circle) bottom. Also comes in 9" and 11".

Opposite page, bottom right:
Heisey close-up of 'Rosette Band' etching.

Heisey 6.125" #1401 'Empress' (called 'Lilies of France' in early ads) dolphin-footed single light candle holders and 9.375" dolphin-footed vase with #448 'Old Colony' plate etching. Candle holders (not etched): sahara, flamingo (most commonly found colors): $325-350 pair; crystal: $265-275 pair; moongleam: $425-450 pair; alexandrite: $550-600 pair. Vase: $250-275 each. (c. 1929-1935). Reissued (1881-1982) by **Imperial** in sunshine yellow and marked 'CG'.

Heisey close-up of #448 'Old Colony' plate etching on vase.

Heisey close-up of cutting on underside of base.

Heisey 7.5" #21 'Aristocrat' single light square candlestick. Crystal with unidentified cutting: $200-250 pair. Also made in 5", 9", 11", and 15". (c. 1907-1935; 1941). Most marked. The 15" was introduced in 1913; the 11" and 15" were discontinued in 1930; the 5" (1909-1910) is the rarest. Found with various etchings and cuttings; also used as a base for lamps, epergnes, and candelabra.

Heisey 9.5" #21 'Aristocrat' four-sided single light candlestick. Crystal with cutting: $200-225 pair; without cutting: $165-175 pair. (1907-1935; 1941).

Heisey 8.785" #3 'Marlboro' hexagonal single light candle holder with six scallops on candle cup, a faceted knob at top of column and molded, serrated edges on the vertical columns. Crystal only: $250-275 pair. (c. 1902-1921). Found with various cuttings. Made in 9" only. Hard to find.

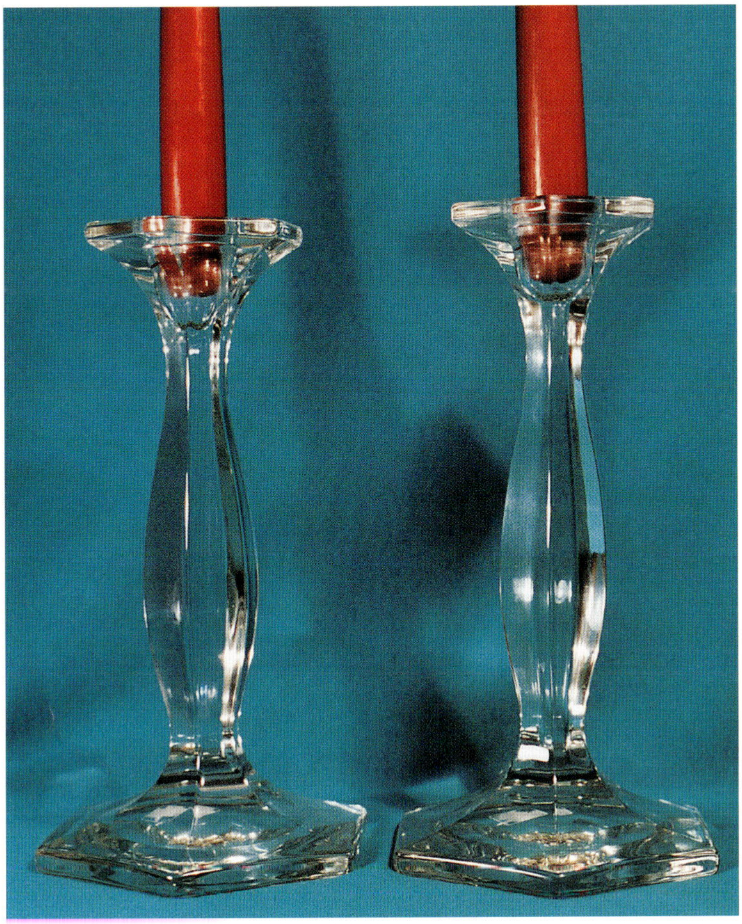

Heisey 8.875" #5 'Patrician' hexagonal single light candle holders. Crystal only: $150-160 pair. (c. 1904-1933). Some marked. Can be found full-cut and full-cut with cut star under base. 'Patrician' also comes in 5" (reissued by **Imperial**), 6", 7", 8", and 11". The **Paden City** #109 is very similar, but has a pressed star on the base.

Heisey 9" #5 'Patrician' six-sided single light candle holder. Crystal with iridized amethyst: $150-160 pair. This color was probably added by another company. Marked.

Heisey 9" #2 'Old Williamsburg' single light hexagonal candle holders with 8.375" 'Twilight' (Germany) kerosene candle inserts (overall 17.25"). Crystal only: $175-190 pair; inserts: $100-110 pair. (c. 1901-1935; 1943). Some marked. The 7" candle holder (1903-1957) was made in crystal and moongleam; the 11" (1902-1931) was made in crystal only. Can be found full cut; was used as the base for candelabra and lamps. **Note**: Jeannette, Lancaster, and Westmoreland made similar candle holders.

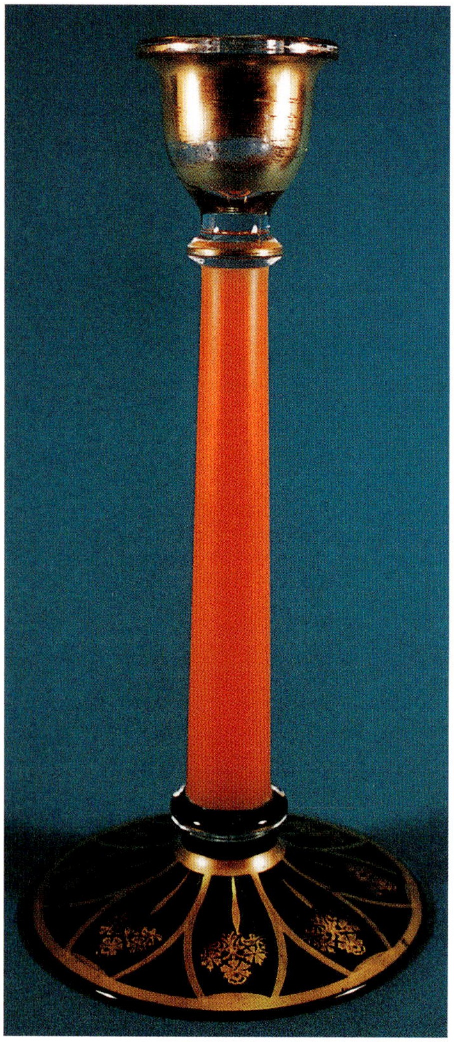

Heisey 9" #100 'Centennial' single light candle holder. Crystal with orange and black decoration with heavy gold on cup, rings, and base: $190-200 pair; without decoration: crystal: $190-200 pair; flamingo: $250-275 pair; moongleam: $275-300 pair. (1920s). Decorated by an unknown firm.

Heisey console set "marriage" with 9" #100 'Centennial' candle holders and **Westmoreland** 10.25" #1041 bowl. Candle holders: $190-200 pair; bowl: $65-75 each.

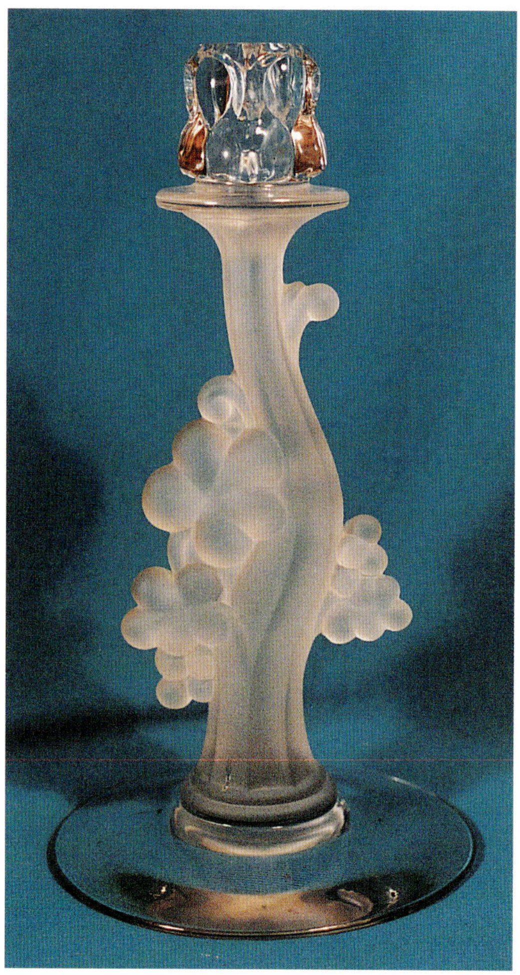

Left:
Heisey 10.125" #1445 'Grape Cluster' single light candle holder. Crystal with crystal satin finish, crystal: $300-325 pair; stiegel blue (cobalt) (rare): $1750-1850 pair. (c. 1935-1944). Most marked. Can be found with cuttings; also comes as a one-light candelabrum with bobeches and prisms.

Right:
Heisey alternate view showing 10.125" #1445 "Grape Cluster' single light candelabrum with #6 bobeche and twelve 'A' prisms used as an electric lamp. Crystal: $275-300 each. (c. 1935-1936). The candle holder is not modified; it has an electric socket inserted into the candle cup and a cloth shade added; assembled by another company.

Heisey close-up of cutting.

Heisey 8.875" #101 'Simplicity' single light candle holder. Crystal with floral cutting: $250-275 pair; no decoration: $200-225 pair. (c. 1922-1929). Made in crystal only. Most marked. Hard to find.

Heisey alternate view showing assembled lamp. This is the original shade.

Heisey 5.125" x 6.5" #1540 'Lariat' double light candle holder. Crystal with heavy silver deposit: $85-95 pair. (c. 1941-1957). Made in crystal only. Reissued by **Imperial** (c. 1958-1968). 'Lariat' was a popular pattern made to compete with **Imperial's** 'Candlewick' pattern.

Below:
Heisey 5.5" #134 'Trident' double light candle holder. Crystal with #504 'Tea Rose' etching: $100-110 pair; without decoration: crystal: $75-80 pair; flamingo: $185-200 pair; moongleam, sahara: $225-240 pair; marigold: $400-450 pair; alexandrite: $750-800 pair. (c. 1929-1957). This candle holder was used extensively for cuttings and etching. It came in various top/foot color combinations: crystal/moongleam, crystal,/dawn, sahara/alexandrite (rare), sahara/moongleam, and tangerine/crystal (rare). Reissued by **Imperial** (c. 1958-1971). The 'Tea Rose' plate etching was used for a console set with #134 'Trident' candle holders and the #1509 'Queen Ann' 11" dolphin-footed floral bowl.

Heisey close-up of #504 'Tea Rose' etching

Heisey 5.625" x 8.75" #1567 'Plantation' double light candle holders with 5.625" x 11.5" footed gardenia bowl. Crystal only. Candle holders: $220-230 pair; bowl: $155-165 each. (c. 1949-1957). Few marked. Can be found with #516 'Plantation Ivy' etching.

Right:
Heisey 7" x 9" #1493 'World' double light art deco candle holder. Crystal only with unidentified cutting: $1250-1350 pair. This is an extensive floral cutting with cut edges on body and base. (c. 1937-1941). Can be found with #893 'Carlton' cutting. Scarce with or without cutting.

Heisey 11" x 12" #402 'Gothic' double light candle holder with two 4" wide #402 bobeches and twenty 'A' prisms. Crystal: $550-600 pair; crystal with stiegel blue foot: $775-800 pair; sahara: $1125-1175 pair; stiegel blue with crystal foot: $1725-1800 pair. (c. 1932-1935). Some marked. Also found with 'C' prisms and with various etchings and satin finishes.

Heisey alternate view.

Heisey 7.5" x 6.75" #142 'Cascade' triple light candle holders. Sahara: $300-325 pair; crystal: $100-110 pair. This candle holder was very popular and was used for numerous cuttings and etchings.

Heisey 7.25" x 6.75" #142 'Cascade' triple light candle holder. Stiegel blue with crystal base: $1000-1050 pair. (c. 1933-1957). Few marked. Hard to find in color. Reissued by **Imperial** (1958-1968).

J. Hoare & Company

Corning, New York, 1868-1920. Brilliant cut glass and fine engraved wares.

Hoare 7.875" #9993 single light skirted candle holder. Crystal with cutting: $250-275 pair. Marked 'J. Hoare & Co'. Shown in 1906-1911 catalogs.

Imperial Glass Company

Bellaire, Ohio, 1901-1973. Sold to **Lenox, Inc.**, closed in 1984. Tableware, pressed ware, and slag glass.

Imperial 1.375" x 4.5" 'Candlewick' low leaf pattern single light candle holders. Doeskin (#1952/170) matte milk glass with pressed leaf pattern and ball edge, pink: $40-45 pair; white milk glass, white carnival glass (#1950/170): $35-40 pair; crystal with cutting or etching: $50-60 pair; ultra blue carnival: $65-70 pair; marigold carnival: $75-80 pair. (c. 1950-1960). Ultra blue carnival and marigold carnival were made for the 1978 convention; white carnival and pink carnival were made for the 1984 convention. (c. 1950-1960).

Imperial 2" line #718R rolled edge single light candle holder with #19 'Appiano' floral cutting. Amber: $60-65 pair; green, Rose Marie: $70-75 pair. These were used in three- or five-piece console sets.

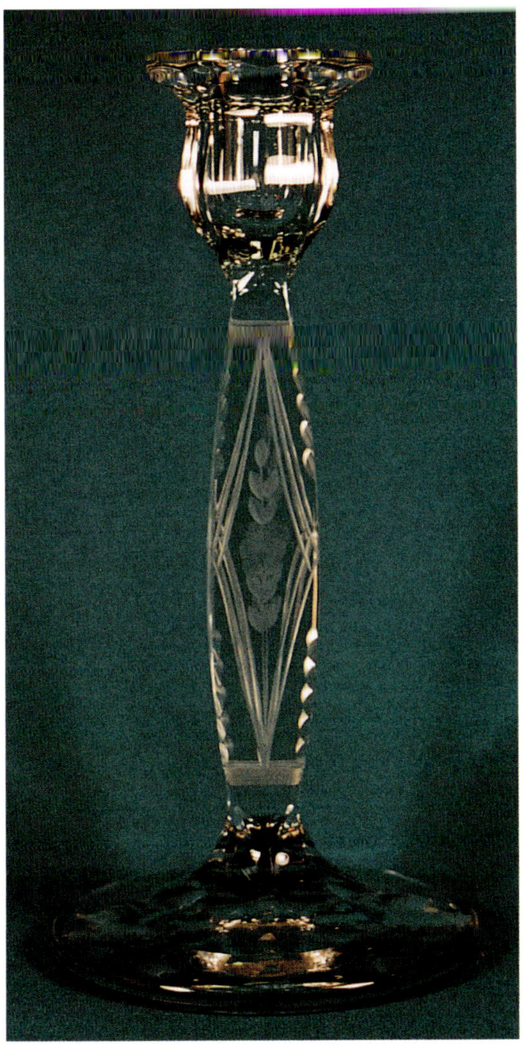

Hoare 9.625" #1192 single light candle holder with four-paneled column and cup with a round base. Crystal with cutting: $250-275 pair. This blank is shown in the 1910 catalog. It predates, but is similar to **Heisey's** #29 which has a round candle cup.

Imperial 2.125" x 3.125" #5020 'Shen' single light candle blocks from the 'Cathay Crystal' line. Frosted crystal: $50-55 pair. Part of a three-piece 'Shen' console set (c. 1949). Reissued in 1960s and 1980s in transparent blue, opaque jade, green, frosted verde, frosted cranberry: $55-60 pair. Possibly made in black and opaque blue.

Imperial 2.5" x 5.25" #505/90 'Collectors Crystal' single light nappy candle holder. Crystal: $45-50 pair; crystal with fired on gold: $70-75 pair; crystal with fired on ruby stain: $95-100 pair. (c. 1960s-1970s).

Imperial 2.625" x 4.25" #1886/285 'Hobnail' square single light candle holder. Vaseline opalescent: $75-80 pair. (c. mid 1960s). Part of 'Stamm House Dew Drop Opalescent' line #1886.

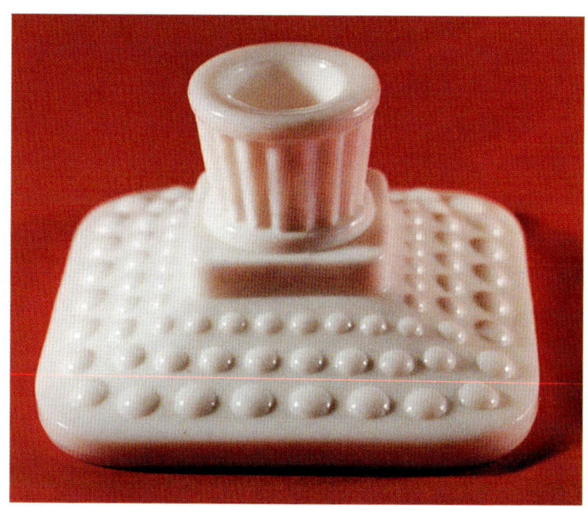

Imperial 2.625" x 4.25" #1950/285 'Hobnail' single light square candle holder. White milk glass: $40-45 pair. (c. 1956-1960).

Imperial 2.375" x 6" #400/40S (square) 'Candlewick Flower' single light candle holder. Crystal: $110-125 pair. (c. 1947-1951). The width varies from 5" to 6" depending on how much of the sides have been turned up.

Imperial 3.25" #637 single light candle holder with swirled pattern pressed under domed base. Crystal with marigold iridescence under base: $70-75 pair. This is an unusual treatment for Imperial as most of their candle holders are iridized on the outer surface. This candle holder may be found with intaglio grape under the base. Hard to find.

Imperial 2.875" x 4.5" #727 single light hexagonal mushroom candle holder. Blue, green, rose: $50-55 pair; crystal: $40-45 pair; amber: $45-50 pair. Used in three- or five-piece console sets.

Imperial close-up of iridescence under candle base.

Imperial 3.375" #880 'Grape' single light candle holder. Slag (ruby only), ruby satin, ruby glossy: $70-75 pair; satin white milk glass, glossy white milk glass: $25-30 pair. (c. 1969-1974).

Imperial (**Heisey** #33 'Toy Skirted Panel') single light candle holder. Sunshine yellow, ruby, stiegel green: $45-50 pair; crystal: $30-35 pair; ultrablue, pink: $40-45 pair. (1981-1984). This candle holder was not made in colors by **Heisey**. **Imperial** reissued about ten pair in ruby in 1982; plus seventy-five pair ultrablue, fifty pair pink, and fifty pair sunshine yellow in 1984 for the Heisey Collector's Association.

Imperial 7.375" x 4.625" #1950/330 single light candle holder. White milk glass (glossy or satin): $40-45 pair; verde, azalea: $45-50 pair. (c. 1955-1960; 1977-1978).

Imperial 6" x 9.75" #1950/196 'Candlewick' single light footed candle/epergne bowl. White milk glass: $70-75 each. With epergne insert (10" tall): $95-100 each. **Note**: This piece is especially nice with vertical ribbing along the fluted edges and pressed grape pattern inside the bowl. A plainer version is shown in one of our earlier books.

Imperial close-up of grape leaf pattern inside bowl.

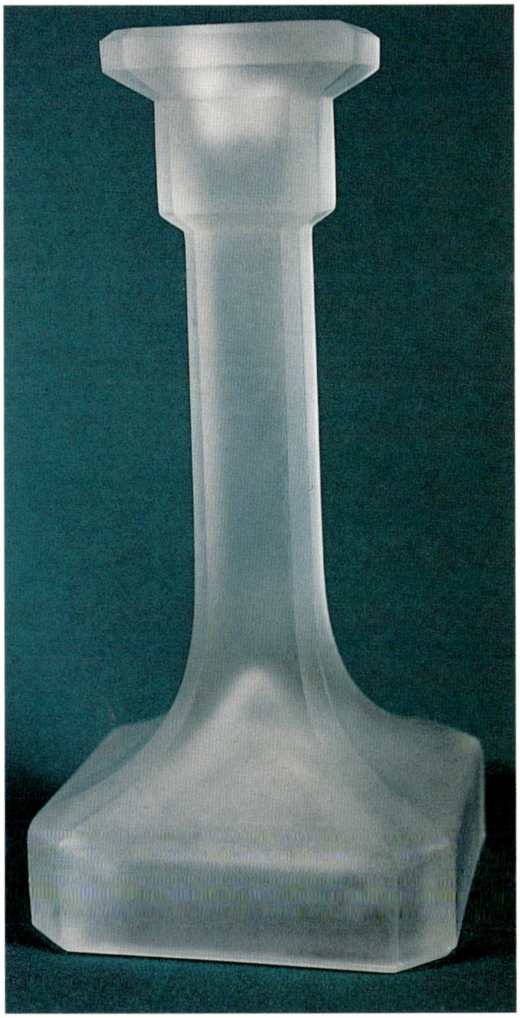

Left:
Imperial 7.375" x 4.5" #6247 single light candle holder with mitered corners from candle cup to base. Crystal satin, crystal: $35-40 pair; green, Rose Marie: $45-50 pair. (c. 1925-1935). Can be found with cuttings and etchings.

Right:
Imperial 8.25" #320 'Double Scroll' single light candlestick. Crystal with #451 rock crystal cutting, amber: $70-75 pair; blue: $80-85 pair; green, Rose Marie: $90-95 pair; golden green, black with gold trim and floral decoration: $100-110 pair. (1920s-1930s).

Left:
Imperial 7.25" #1952/80 'Vinelf' single light candle holder. Doeskin milk glass, white milk glass: $50-55 pair; verde, crystal: $40-45 pair; transparent satin colors: antique blue, cranberry: $45-50 pair; turquoise blue milk glass, green milk glass, custard milk glass: $60-65 pair; black with gold decoration, black suede: $75-80 pair. (c. 1950-1965). The mold is currently owned by **L.E. Smith**.

Right:
Imperial 8.375" 'Double Scroll' single light candle stick. Rose Marie with #457 rock crystal cutting: $90-95 pair.

Imperial 8.125" x 10.5" 'Two Handled' (originally called 'Grecian') single light candle bowl. Peacock iridescent/rose ice (marigold stretch) combination of carnival and stretch: $200-225 each; blue ice (blue smoke): $250-275 each. (c. 1920s). Hard to find.

Imperial 8.5" 'Premium' single light candle holder with twist optic base. Rubigold (marigold) iridescent: $90-95 pair.

Imperial 7.75" x 10" 'Two Handled' single light candle bowl. Rubigold iridescent/iris ice (pearl stretch) combination of carnival and stretch: $200-225 each. (c. 1920s). Hard to find.

Imperial alternate view showing both candle bowls together.

Imperial 8.875" #5172 'Dolphin' single light candle holder. Nut brown (1976-1977), ultra blue, green, amber: $85-90 pair. (c. 1970s). White milk glass (#1950/90): $70-75 pair. (c. 1954-1958; 1977-1978).

Imperial 5" x 8" #752 heart-shaped double light candle holder. Crystal with cutting: $80-85 pair. (c. 1934-1951). This also came as the #752 candelabra with bobeche and candle pegs as part of a three-piece console set #84BX/752 which used a 15" bowl. The 2 added to #75 denotes a two-light candle holder.

Imperial close-up of cutting

Imperial for **Metropolitan Museum of Art** 11" K-15 'Sandwich Dolphin' single light candle holder. Stiegel green, sky blue: $100-115 pair; crystal: $85-90 pair. (c.1974-1981). Marked 'MMA'.

Imperial 6.625" x 8" #753 triple light candle holder. Stiegel green, Ritz blue: $150-160 pair; crystal, white milk glass (1950/75): $135-145 pair; ruby: $165-175 pair. (c. 1934-1951). This was the first triple candle holder made by **Imperial**. This candle holder was used extensively for cuttings, and it was used in console sets.

Imperial console set with 6.625" x 8" #75 or #753 triple light candle holders and 12.75" flanged four-footed bowl. Stiegel green: $190-200 set.

Indiana Glass Company

Dunkirk, Indiana, 1907 to present. Tableware and gift items.

Indiana console set with 3.75" x 4.5" #603 single light candle holders and 13.25" bowl. Crystal with yellow, white and silver decoration: $70-80 set.

Indiana 3.625" x 4.375" #603 single light candle holders with various decorations. Pink with decoration, green with decoration: $40-45 pair; crystal with decoration: $35-40 pair.

Indiana 3.625" x 4.375" #603 single light candle holders with various decorations: $35-45 pair.

Indiana 3.875" #172 single light candle holder. Crystal with yellow, gold and white decoration: $35-40 pair; no decoration: crystal, amber: $25-30 pair; green $30-35 pair. (c. 1920s). This blank was also used for 'Old English' or 'Threading'.

Indiana 5" single light candle holder with triangular base. Teal, yellow, amber, green: $18-22 pair. Can be found with various flashed colors.

Indiana 4.5" x 4.625" bell-shaped double light candle holder. Crystal with pressed fruit design with bananas: $80-85 pair. These candle holders are made of good quality glass. Although we have seen fired on colors on bowls, we have seen the candle holders in crystal only.

Indiana 6" x 3.75" 'Tiara Exclusives' single light 'Sandwich Glo Lamp.' Peach, spruce, chantilly green, bicentennial blue (c. 1976): $25-30 each; amber: $20-25 each; ruby (c. early 1970s): $40-45 each. These lamps were sold as singles.

Above right:
Indiana 5.5" x 6.25" 'Garland' double light candle holder. Crystal with blue, green and fuchsia fired on color: $75-80 pair. Candle holders from this mold were made of good quality glass for major department stores. (c. 1930s).

Right:
Indiana 5.25" x 6.25" 'Garland' double light candle holders. Crystal with frosted bases, crystal with frosted garland ring: $70-75 pair; crystal: $65-70 pair. (c. 1930s).

Indiana 5.25" x 6.25" 'Garland' double light candle holder. Crystal with ruby stained base, crystal with ruby stained garland ring: $75-80 pair; crystal with amber stained garland ring: $70-75 pair. (c. 1930s).

Italy

Italy 3.375" x 3.875" single light candle holder with domed base. Crystal: $20-25 pair. Three-part mold. Paper 'Hand-made in Italy' label.

Italy 6.5" single light art glass fish candle holder. Crystal/green: $40-45 pair.

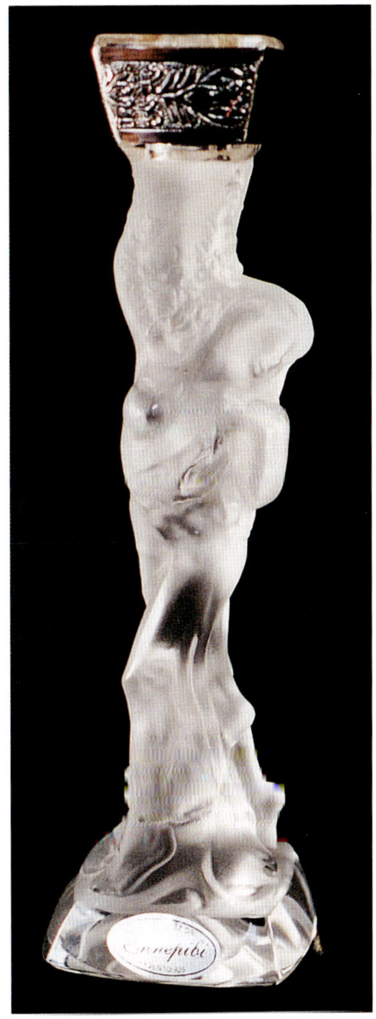

Italy 8" #T/12121 figural single light candle holder. Crystal/crystal satin with silver tape decoration: $185-195 pair. Marked 'Ennepibi'.

Left:
Italy 9.125" single light candle holder. Blue: $250-275 pair.

Right:
Italy (Venetian) 9.375" single light candle holder with flared drip plate. Green: $400-450 pair. Came as a set of four.

Italy (Venetian) 10" single light two-piece candle holder. Pink with gold fleck: $250-275 pair.

Italy alternate view.

Italy console set with 10.625" single light candle holders and 13" bowl: $1800-2000 set.

Italy 10.625" single light candle holder with glass finial (total 13.5"). Cranberry/crystal with applied colored glass flowers: $1200-1300 pair.

Italy close up of applied glass flowers.

Italy 13.5" alternate view with glass finials.

Italy close-up of finial.

Italy alternate view with all parts assembled.

Right:
Italy 10.375" single light candle holder. Amethyst with applied crystal accents: $250-275 pair.

Italy (Venetian) 11.625" single light candlestick with separate drip plate. Light green with gold fleck: $2000-2250 pair.

Italy alternate view.

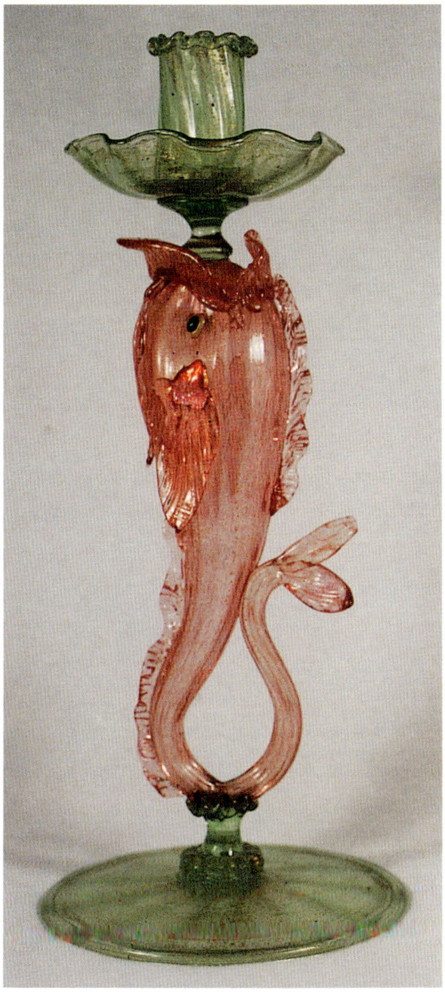

Italy (Venetian) 12.5" x 5.25" dolphin single light candle holder. Pink and green with gold flecks: $2250-2500 pair.

Italy alternate view showing table center: $5000-5500 set.

Italy (Venetian) 7.875" x 10" compote with dolphin head candle holders. Pink and green with gold flecks: $2500-2750 each.

Italy 17" and 15" 'Shinted Urn' spiral single light candle pillars with applied candle cups. Crystal: 15": $260-275 pair; 17": $325-350 pair; 19": $340-365 pair; and 21": $375-400 pair.

Italy (Venetian) 9.75" x 12.25" with 7" wide base double light candle holder with glass flower finial. Crystal, green, and rust with gold fleck accents: $2500-3000 pair.

Italy (Murano) 22" single light candle pillar. Crystal with gold fleck and eyes: $950-1050 pair.

Italy alternate view of glass flower finial.

Lancaster Glass Company

Lancaster, Ohio, 1908-1924. Became a subsidiary of **Hocking Glass Company** and continues production. Cut and decorated tableware.

Lancaster 2.5" #355 single light candle holders. Green, topaz: $35-40 pair. (c. 1932).

Lancaster 8.25" x 4.5" #984 single light candle holder. Dark amber with black and gold trim: $35-40 pair.

Lancaster 8.5" #904 single light candlestick. Fired on colors: orange, red, canary, green, blue (some decorated with black or gold): $35-40 pair.

Left:
Lancaster 6.5" single light candle holder. Crystal (turned light amethyst by sun): $60-65 pair. Price is for crystal in mint condition. (c. 1922). This candle holder is similar to **Heisey's** #2 'Old Williamsburg', but has a shorter more flared candle cup.

Lancaster 9.5" single light candlesticks. Black with hand decoration: $95-100 pair.

Lancaster 1.75" x 7" 'Dogwood' double light candle block. Crystal with fired on colors and gold centers and candle rims: blue, pink, amethyst, red: $70-75 pair; crystal with satin flowers: $55-60 pair.

L.E. Smith Glass Company

Mt. Pleasant, Pennsylvania. 1907 to present. Black glass.

L.E. Smith 3.125" x 5" #27 candle holder. Crystal with black applied floral decoration: $30-35 pair. The base is flatter than on many #27s.

L.E. Smith showing alternate decoration.

3511 **L.E. Smith** 3" #27 single light candle holders. Black with floral decoration: $35-40 pair. (c. 1920s).

L.E. Smith 4.75" x 4" #6661A single light angel on star candle holder. Light teal, amber: $35-40 pair; crystal, crystal satin: $30-35 pair; almond nouveau slag (c. 1980-1981): $60-65 pair.

L.E. Smith console set with 3.125" x 5" candle holders and 11.75" bowl: $50-60 set. Notice that the candle holders are not identical and that the bowl incorporates both designs. The original console set undoubtedly had four candle holders, two of each design.

L.E. Smith 5.75" x 8" #65 swan single light candle holder. Crystal: $30-35 pair. Also made in almond nouveau slag as a dish.

L.E. Smith 7.625" x 5" 'Moon & Stars' three-piece fairy light. Orange/crystal: $25-30 each.

L.E. Smith alternate view.

L.E. Smith 7.625" x 5" 'Moon & Stars' three-piece fairy light. Green opalescent: $25-30 each.

L.G. Wright

New Martinsville, West Virginia, 1937-1999. Colonial and Victorian reproductions of lamps and glassware.

L.G. Wright alternate view. Sparkling ruby (red iridescent): $130-140 pair.

L.G. Wright (derived from an old **Northwood** mold) 5" #3-1 'No. 3 Beaded' single light candle holder. Stormy blue (blue iridescent), sparkling ruby (red iridescent) (both c. 1995): $130-140 pair; crystal (c. 1990-1991): $110-120 pair; vaseline (c. 1960s): $140-150 pair; vaseline opalescent: $165-175 pair; ruby: $190-200 pair.

L.G. Wright alternate view. Ruby: $190-200 pair.

Libbey

New England Glass Works: W.L. Libbey & Son Company, Cambridge, Massachusetts, 1878-1888. Moved to Toledo, Ohio, in 1988 and became **Libbey Glass Company**, 1890-1936. Was absorbed in 1936 by **Owen-Illinois, Incorporated**, 1936-present. Largest cut glass factory in the world during the Brilliant Cut Glass period.

Libbey 6" 'Drape' cut crystal single light hollow candle holder. Crystal: $700-750 pair.

Libbey alternate view.

Libbey 10" (11.375" on wooden stand) tear drop stemmed single light candle holder. Crystal with #1080 engraving: $850-900 pair.

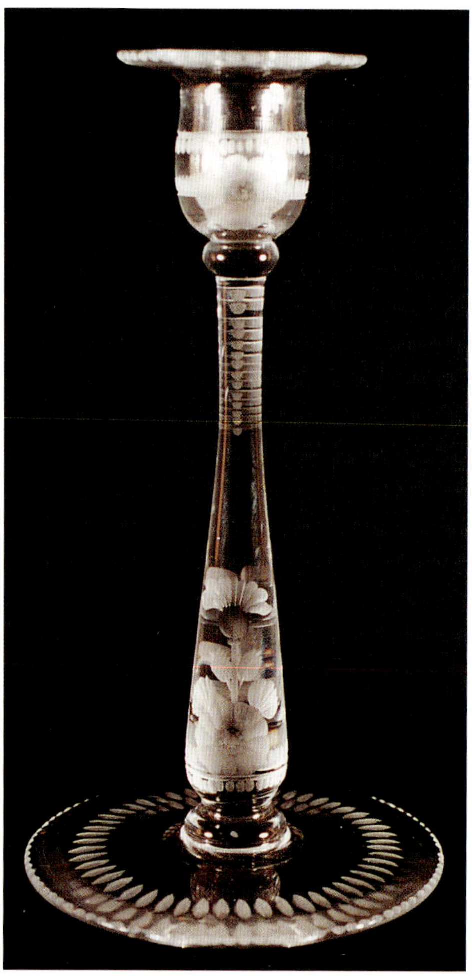

Libbey 8" single light candle holder with floral engraving. Crystal: $600-650 pair.

McKee Glass Company

Jeannette, Pennsylvania, 1900-1951. Tableware, kitchen ware, and gift items.

McKee 3.125" #200 single light candle holder. Rose pink with cutting: $30-35 pair. (c. 1930s). We have seen this hexagonal base only in pink. Can be found with various cuttings, etchings, and gold encrustations.

McKee 8" #154 single light candelabra with #126 cutting on base and stem. Crystal only: $190-200 pair. This is from **McKee's** 'Stone Engraved Ware' assortment. These candle holders were part of a three-piece console set and had various cuttings.

McKee 5.5" 'Rock Crystal' or 'Early American Rock Crystal' single light candle dish with pressed floral and scroll pattern. Crystal: $45-50 pair; amberina, canary yellow, amethyst, pink, aquamarine, four shades of green, milk glass, red slag (some with satin finish): $70-80 pair; cobalt: $160-170 pair; red: $215-225 pair. (c. 1920s-1930s).

McKee alternate view of pressed pattern.

McKee 9.75" single light crucifix candle holder with 3.25" crossbar. White milk glass: $200-250 pair. (c. 1894). Note: We have identified this as **McKee** based on W. Heacock's article, "Religious Figures in Glass."

McKee 8.25" 'Rock Crystal' or 'Early American Rock Crystal' single light candle holder with pressed floral design. Amber: $165-175 pair; crystal: $100-110 pair; cobalt: $350-375 pair; red: $450-475 pair; other colors: $165-175 pair. (c. 1920s-1930s).

Right:
McKee 9" #151 single light candle holder. Cobalt: $250-275 pair; crystal: $140-150 pair. (c. 1920s). Note the two rings at the top and bottom of the column making this candle holder different from those of **Tiffin** and **Cambridge**, both of which have only one ring at top and bottom. Part of the #151-A console set. Possibly found in other colors.

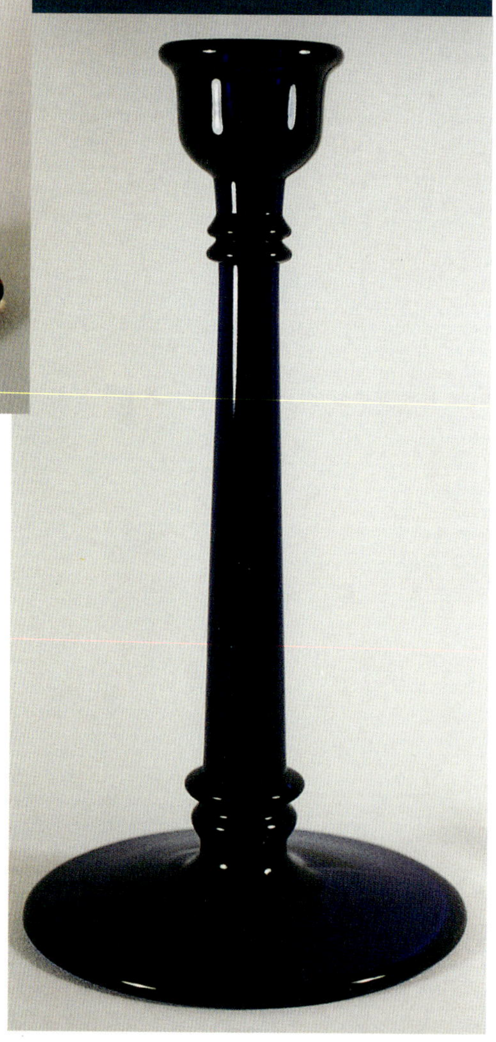

C.F. Monroe Company

Meriden, Connecticut, 1880-1916. Cut glass and glass decorating.

Monroe 8.5" single light candle holder. Crystal with cuttings: $250-275 pair. (c. early 1900s).

Morgantown Glass Works

Morgantown, West Virginia,. Late 1800s-1903 became **Economy Tumbler Company**; 1929-1937, became **Morgantown Glass Works** again; 1939-1965, became **Morgantown Glassware Guild**; sold to **Fostoria Glass Company** in 1965. Pressed ware, blown ware, and blanks for many other companies.

Left:
Morgantown 8.75" #104 'Coronet' single light candle lamps. Gypsy fire (introduced in 1962): $95-100 pair; ebony (#1300; introduced in 1966): $70-75 pair; ruby: $125-150 pair. May come in other colors. (c. 1960s). Paper labels.

Right:
Morgantown 10.375" #37 'Emperor' single light candle holder/vase in spiral optic. 14K topaz with green base: $350-375 pair. (c. 1920s).

New England Glass Co.

Boston Porcelain and Glass Company, East Cambridge Massachusetts, 1814-1817; **New England Glass Company**, 1817-1888. Moved to Toledo, Ohio in 1888 and became **Libbey Glass Company** in 1890. Tableware, novelty items, and "Mercury Glass."

Metropolitan Museum of Art (reissue of a **New England Glass** mold) 7.5" single light candlestick. 7" colors: deep blue, sea green (possibly others): $75-80 pair. Marked 'MMA'. Colors for 9" (original mold, c. 1850-1888): rose amethyst, canary, clam broth (translucent white), crystal, vaseline, grass green, sapphire blue, greenish blue: $650-700 pair; shown in "Designs from New England Catalogue of Pressed Glass" (c. 1869).

Left:
Metropolitan Museum of Art (reissue of a **New England Glass** mold) 7.5" single light candlestick. Rose amethyst: $75-80 pair. Marked 'MMA'. These have been reproduced in pink and blue by **Castle Antiques and Reproductions, Inc.**, but are very poor glass.

Right:
New England Glass 7.25" 'Mercury Glass' or Silver Glass' single light candle holder. Mercury glass with flower decoration: $750-800 pair. Mercury Glass was patented by the New England Glass Company in 1855. It was made by sandwiching a layer of silver color between two cased crystal layers.

New England Glass 9" hexagonal single light candle holder. Crystal: $375-400 pair. (c. 1870-1880). One-piece mold. Has been reproduced in 9.25" from a two-piece mold.

Left:
New England Glass 7.875" single light candle holder. Clam broth (translucent white milk glass): $375-400 pair. Shown in the "New England Catalogue of Pressed Glass" (c. 1869). Made in 7.5" and 9.5". This candle holder was reissued in crystal as '#3 Candlestick' by **Hobbs, Brockunier** (c. late 1870s).

Right:
New England Glass 9.375" 'Mercury glass' or 'Silver Glass' single light candle holder. Mercury glass: $400-450 pair.

New England Glass 10.25" 'Mercury Glass' or 'Silver Glass' single light candle holder with ruffled glass collar. Mercury glass: $800-900 pair.

New England Glass 9.5" #1136 'Crucifix' single light candle holder with 3.625" x 1.25" cross-arm. White milk glass: $950-1050 pair; blue transparent, green transparent: $1500-1600 pair. (c. 1868).

Boston & Sandwich 11.5" single light crucifix candle holder with 4.25" cross-arm. Opaque white: $1200-1250 pair; pink (rare), emerald green, intense blue-green citron, translucent medium blue, translucent powder blue: cannot price. (c. 1860-1865). All very scarce. The 'INRI' banner on this candle holder is not curved as is the one made by **Co-Operative Flint**.

New Martinsville

New Martinsvillle, West Virginia. 1901-1944. Sold and reorganized as **Viking Glass Company**. Innovative table lines and gift items.

New Martinsville 2" x 4.75" #37 'Moon Drops' single light candle holder. Amethyst: $50-55 pair; amber, crystal: $30-35 pair; black, evergreen, jade, rose: $45-50 pair; ruby, cobalt: $55-60 pair. (c. 1932-1940s). Note the straight edge.

New Martinsville 3.875" #970 single light candle holder. Crystal with silver cup and trim and silver encrusted floral etching: $45-50 pair. (c. 1930s-1940s). The top of the candle cup is cut and polished. **Viking** reissued this candle holder in crystal and colors.

New Martinsville 4.5" 'Colonial' single light chamber stick with blue bonnet decoration (found in Texas). White milk glass with decoration: $30-35 pair; white milk glass without decoration, amber: $20-25 pair; green, pink: $25-30 pair. (c. 1933-1937).

New Martinsville/Dalzell 4.25" #5213 single light candle holder with silver edges and silver floral decoration on base. Crystal only: $35-40 pair. (c. 1930s-1950s).

New Martinsville 5.125" x 5.75" 'Sweet Heart Swan' single light candle holder. Ruby with crystal, cobalt with crystal: $140-150 pair; emerald with crystal, black with crystal: $115-125 pair.

New Martinsville 'Sweetheart Swan' three-piece table center with 5.125" candle bowls and 11" center bowl. Cobalt with crystal: $235-250 set.

Below:
New Martinsville 5.25" #37 'Moon Drops' single light candle holders. Ruby: $250-275 pair. Rare. We have not found these in any other color.

New Martinsville/Viking 5.375" #11 single light candle holder. Ruby, cobalt: $35-40 pair; crystal: $25-30 pair (c. early 1900s); cranberry mist: $30-35 pair. **Viking** reissued. (1980s-1990s).

New Martinsville 5.375" #37/2 'Moon Drops' winged single light candle holder. Ruby, cobalt: $110-120 pair; crystal, amber: $60-65 pair; any other 'Moon Drops' color: $70-75 pair. (c. 1932-1940s).

New Martinsville 5" #4457 double light candle holders with #104 cutting. Crystal: $80-85 pair. (c. early 1940s). Reissued by **Viking** (c. 1945-1986). Crystal: $70-75 pair; pale blue: $100-110 pair; ruby: $140-150 pair.

New Martinsville 6.5" #169 single light candle holder. Crystal only with yellow under base and floral decoration, crystal with other decorations: $30-35 pair. (c. 1918-1937). This was **J. B. Higbee Glass Co.** Mold #C-169 (1907-1917). The **Higbee** 'Bee' trademark in one corner of the bottom of the base was removed when **New Martinsville** began production.

New Martinsville close-up of #104 cutting.

New Martinsville close-up of alternate unidentified cutting.

New Martinsville 5.5" x 7" #18 'Eagle' winged double light candle holder. Ruby: $150-175 pair; crystal $100-110 pair. (c. 1936-1944). We have not seen this in any other colors.

New Martinsville 6.5" x 7.5" #42 'Radiance' double light candle holder with large fanned circle panel. Amber: $95-100 pair; crystal : $90-95 pair; pink, emerald green: $100-125 pair; ruby, cobalt, ice blue: $175-185 pair. (c. 1936-1944).

New Martinsville 5.25" x 7" #37/3 'Moon Drops' winged triple light candle holders and 5.25" #37/2 single light candle holder. Triple light: ruby, cobalt: $160-175 pair; crystal: $95-100 pair; other colors: $100-125 pair. Single light: ruby: $110-120 pair.

H. Northwood & Company

Wheeling, West Virginia, 1901-1925. Iridescent ware and lighting.

Northwood 3" x 5.5" #675 single light chamber stick. Coral, jade, russet: $135-145 pair; russet stretch: $190-200 pair; blue stretch: $210-220 pair; topaz stretch: $225-235 pair. (c. 1920s). Part of the 'Rainbow Line'.

Right:
Northwood 6.5" #565 'Petticoat Dolphin' single light candle holder. Canary opal: $475-500 pair; flint opal (crystal): $375-400 pair; blue opal: $550-575 pair. Shown in a **Pitkin & Brooks** 1900 catalog of 10-15 cent counter goods.

Northwood flared 'Simple Simon' compote used as single light candle holder/ vase. Green opalescent: $75-80 each; blue opalescent: $80-85 each; white opalescent: $60-65 each. A candle fits into the throat perfectly. This compote is known to carnival collectors as 'Graceful'. (c. 1908-1909).

Northwood alternate view. Blue opalescent: $80-85 each.

Northwood alternate view showing very heavy opalescence.

Left:
Northwood 6.5" #719 single light trumpet candle holders. Chinese coral with gold rings, black, marigold iridescent: $115-125 pair; jade: $100-110 pair; topaz iridescent: $125-135 pair; blue iridescent: $135-145 pair. (c. 1920s). Part of the 'Rainbow Line'.

Northwood 6.875" #658 single light candle holder. Jade blue iridescent: $140-150 pair; blue iridescent, russet iridescent: $100-110 pair; topaz iridescent: $125-135 pair; blue, russet: $85-90 pair; jade green: $95-100 pair; jade blue, topaz: $110-120 pair. (1920s). Part of the 'Rainbow Line'.

Northwood 8.25" #657 single light candle holder. Topaz: $140-150 pair; blue: $100-120 pair; russet: $115-125 pair. Part of the 'Rainbow Line'.

Northwood 8.375" #657 single light candle holder. Jade with gold trim: $110-115 pair; tan coral (variation of Chinese coral): $95-100 pair; jade blue: $125-135 pair; Chinese coral: $130-140 pair; ivory (custard) iridescent (scarce): $185-200 pair. Part of the 'Rainbow Line'.

Northwood 8.5" #657 single light candle holder. Russet iridescent: $125-135 pair; blue iridescent: $115-125 pair; topaz iridescent: $150-160 pair; dark amethyst iridescent (scarce): $325-350 pair. Part of the 'Rainbow Line'.

Ohio Flint Glass Company

Lancaster, Ohio. Tableware and novelty items. **Jefferson Glass Company**, Steubenville, Ohio, 1900-1907; Follensbee, West Virginia, 1907-?

Ohio Flint/Jefferson/Central 6.625" #310 'Chippendale' single light 'KRYS-TOL' candle holder. Crystal (turned light amethyst by sun): $165-175 pair. (c. 1919). **Note**: The **Ohio Flint Glass Co.** had the 'Chippendale' molds from 1907-1909; then the **Jefferson Glass Co.** had them from 1909-1919; **Central Glass Works** purchased all of the line and the copyright for "KRYS-TOL" in 1919. Much of this line had been and continued to be exported to England; this candle holder is shown in an English ad in 1913 and again in 1924. In 1933, **George Davidson & Co.** in England purchased the molds for the complete line of 'Chippendale'; the designation 'KRYS-TOL' did not appear in his 1933 ad.

Ohio Flint/Jefferson/Central 6.625" #310 'Chippendale' single light 'KRYS-TOL' candle holder. Crystal: $200-225 pair. This candle holder was shown in a **Central** ad in 1924 as #T-310 as part of a trinket (dresser) set; in the same ad, the #310 was also shown made with a square candle cup with rings at both top and bottom.

Ohio Flint/Jefferson/Central table center with 6.625" #310 'Chippendale' single light 'KRYS-TOL' candle holders and 8.5" x 6.75" compote. Crystal: $450-500 set. Marked 'Patent pending FEB 5, 1907' . The compote is made from the #310 candle holder and a bowl shown in a **Jefferson** ad in 1913.

Ohio Flint/Jefferson/Central 9.375" 'Chippendale' trophy style single light candle holder. Vaseline: $400-450 pair. **Note**: 'KRYS-TOL' was a trademark for a quality of glass and can be found in other pattern lines.

Ohio Flint/Jefferson/Central 8.75" 'Chippendale' hexagonal single light 'KRYS-TOL' candle holder. Crystal: $400-450 pair. This candle holder, shown in a **Jefferson** ad in 1913, is a beautiful fire polished line of 'Colonial' style crystal; there are several different styles of candle holders in this line.

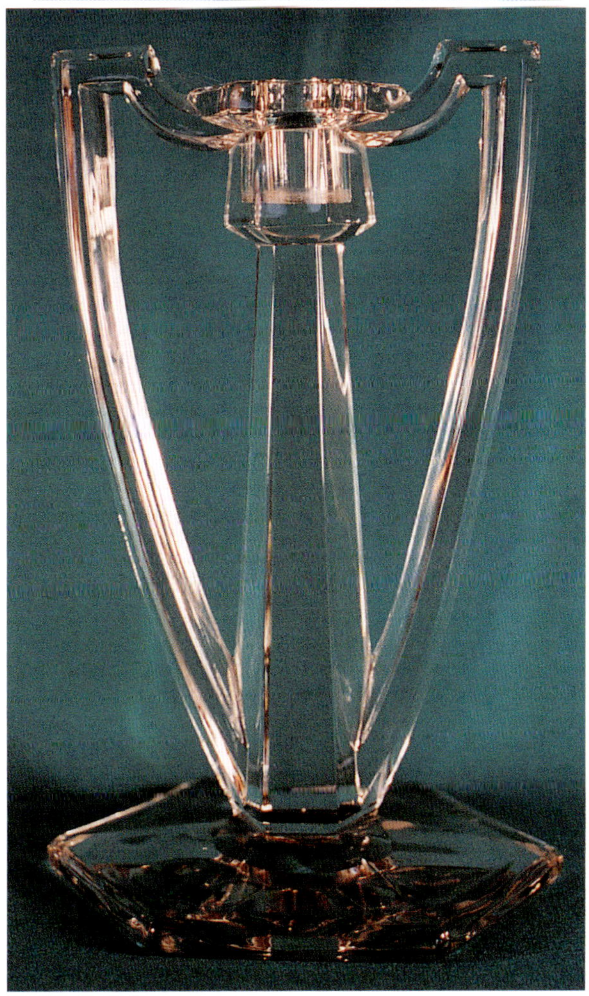

Ohio Flint/Jefferson/Central 9.375" 'Chippendale' trophy style single light candle holder. Crystal: $400-450 pair. Marked 'KRYS-TOL'.

Paden City Glass Manufacturing Company

Paden City, West Virginia, 1916-1951. Pressed tableware and occasional ware.

Right:
Paden City 2.5" #531 (for **Van Deman & Son** on **Paden City's** #210 'Regina' blank) single light candle holder with deer etching; part of the 'Black Forest' line. Amber: $80-85 pair; pink, green: $125-135 pair; crystal: $70-75 pair; black: $160-170 pair; black with white-gold bands or gold encrustation: $190-200 pair. (c. 1928-1930s).

Paden City close-up of deer etching.

Paden City 2.5" #701 single light mushroom candle holder. Amber with gold deposit, ebony with gold: $45-50 pair; crystal with gold: $35-40 pair; cheriglo (pink) with gold, green with gold: $50-55 pair. (c. 1920s). This candle holder was used for many different decorations and etchings.

Paden City close-up of gold deposit.

Paden City 2.75" #300 line #1503 single light candle holder. Crystal with unknown cutting: $35-40 pair; crystal with cranberry stain: $45-50 pair. (c. 1930s-1940s). We have seen this candle holder in crystal only.

Paden City close-up of cutting.

Paden City 3.25" #192 single light candle holder. Crystal with unidentified gold-filled etching, amber: $25-30 pair; cheriglo (pink), green: $30-35 pair. (c. 1920s).

Paden City 6.125" single light lustre candle holder shown here with same etching. Crystal with gold decoration and rims: $55-60 pair.

Paden City close-up of etching.

Paden City 3.5" #113 toy single light candle holder. Crystal with star pattern pressed on bottom of base: $35-40 pair. (c. 1920s). Also made in 5.5", 7" and 8.5".

Paden City 5" x 5.5" #412 square, footed single light keyhole candle holder. Topaz with deep etching: $100-125 pair. The base is flattened rather than domed as usual.

Paden City close-up of etching.

Paden City 5.125" #412 single light candle holder, Cobalt with 'Sterling' silver deposit: $85-90 pair.

Paden City close-up of silver deposit.

Paden City close-up of silver deposit.

Paden City 6" 'Butterfly' single light candle holder. Crystal with silver deposit: $65-70 pair. (c. 1930s). This candle holder was used for various etchings, cuttings, and decorations. It can be found in ruby: $165-200 pair, depending on the decoration.

Paden City 6.5" #330 'Rib and Bead' (*reproduction*) single light candle holder. Red: $40-45 pair. Note lack of holes for prisms in side pieces. Originally came in crystal: $80-85 pair; it was used for various etchings such as 'Frost'.

Paden City 6.125" x 4.75" #881 'Gadroon' single light candle holders. Amber with plate etching on base and column: $75-80 pair; ruby without decoration: $115-125 pair. (c. 1930s).

Paden City close-up of plate etching.

Paden City #890 'Crows Foot' console set with 7" single light candle holders and 11" #890 three-footed console bowl. Crystal with cutting: candle holders: $85-90 pair; bowl: $45-50 each. (c. 1930s).

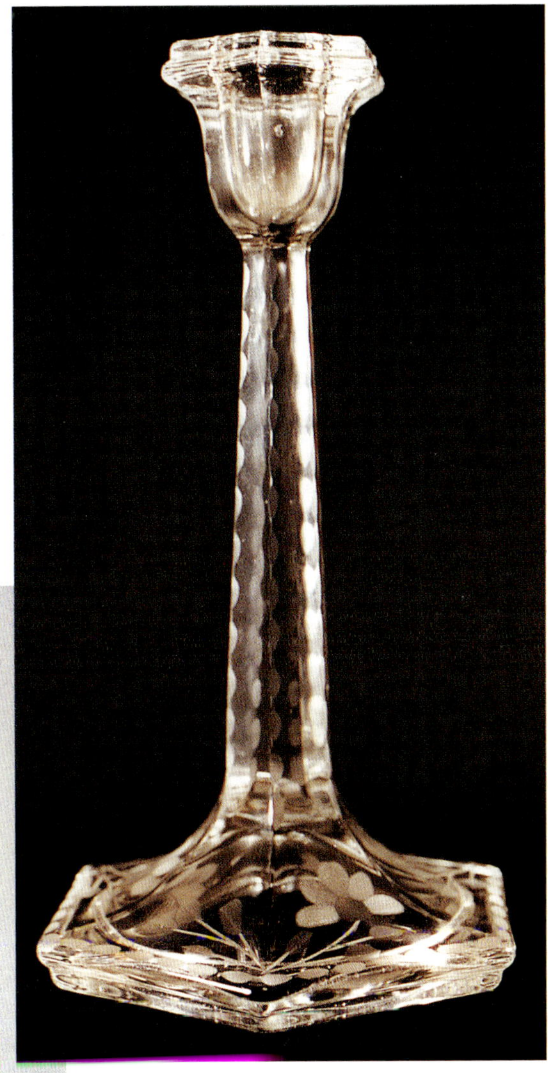

Paden City 9.125" #115 single light candlestick with large hexagonal base. Crystal with notched cuttings on column and floral cutting on base: $75-80 pair. (c. 1920s). Comes in most **Paden City** colors, but is most often seen in crystal and various ambers.

Paden City 9" #115 single light candle holder with horizontal and notched cuttings. Amber: $75-80 pair. **Note**: Both **New Martinsville** and **Fostoria** made 9" sticks virtually identical to these; however, this is one of **Paden City's** unique ambers, and they used various horizontal and notched cuttings on columns. Also comes in 7".

Paden City close-up of cuttings on column.

Paden City 5.175" #444 'Vale' double light candle holders with cutting. Crystal: $85-90 pair. (c. 1930s-1940s). Made to compete with **Imperial's** 'Candlewick'; this candle holder was used for various cuttings and etchings such as 'Gazebo'.

Paden City close-up of cutting.

Paden City 5.25" x 7.25" 'Gadroon' double light candle holder. Blue: $140-150 pair; crystal: $95-100 pair. Usually found in crystal; was used for various etchings and cuttings such as 'Frost'.

Paden City 5.75" #555 double light candle holder. Crystal with floral etching: $125-135 pair. (c. 1930s). We have seen this in crystal only. Used for decorations, cuttings and etchings such as 'Gazebo'.

Paden City close-up of etching.

Below:
Paden City (**Glastonbury/Lotus**) 6" x 6.5" double light candle holder. Crystal with gold encrusted etching #0906 'Bridal Bouquet' and gold decoration on candle rim and base: $65-70 pair. (c. 1930s). We have seen this candle holder in crystal only with various decorations.

Paden City alternate view showing a different **Glastonbury** decoration: $55-60 pair. (c. 1930s). Paper label.

Paden City alternate view of etching.

Paden City 6" x 6.5" double light candle holder. Crystal with ruby stained floral pattern etched-to-clear: $85-90 pair.

Paden City close-up of etching.

Paden City #890 'Crows Foot' fan-shaped triple light candle holder. Amber with deep plate etching: $115-125 pair; crystal: $100-110 pair; cheriglo (pink), green, black: $165-175 pair; ruby, cobalt: $225-250 pair.

Paden City close-up of etching.

Pairpoint Manufacturing Company

New Bedford, Massachusetts, 1880-1900. **Pairpoint Corporation**, 1900-1938. Became **Gunderson Glass Works**, 1939-1952; became **Gunderson-Pairpoint Glass Works**, 1952-1957. Moved to Wareham, Massachusetts during 1957-1958 and became **Pairpoint Glass Company, Incorporated**. Moved to Spain 1958-1970. Moved to Sagamore, Massachusetts as the **Pairpoint Glass Company**, 1970-present. Free- and mold-blown wares, colored glass, and art glass.

Authors' note: **Pairpoint** sold many blanks to other companies and bought blanks from other companies as well. Consequently, one may find **Pairpoint** blanks with other companies' decorations and **Pairpoint** decorations on other companies' blanks.

Pairpoint 3.75" x 4.25" #1640 single light candle holder with domed base. Crystal with rock crystal 'Hempstead' engraving: $500-550 pair.

Pairpoint 2.625" x 3.75" single light rolled edge candle holder. Aurora (amber) with 'Grapes' engraving: $350-375 pair.

Pairpoint 4.25" single light bubble stem candle holder. Aurora (amber): $225-250 pair; cobalt: $325-350 pair.

Pairpoint alternate view.

Pairpoint 8" single light candle holder with spiral air trap in column. Crystal with red and white spiral: $550-600 pair. The column of this stick is used for the #1815 comport; this stick does not have the usual 'Veniti' engraving on the base, but does have a deep radiant cut.

Pairpoint 7.875" single light candle holder with ball connector. Green with bubble ball: $485-535 pair. Has pontil mark.

Pairpoint 9.625" single light candle holder with 'Grapes' engraving. Chrysopras: $1050-1100 pair. This form can be found with a crystal bubble ball.

Pairpoint close-up of 'Grapes' engraving.

Left:
Pairpoint 10" #1627 single light candle holder with a twist panel. Amethyst: $450-500 pair. Has ground pontil mark.

Pairpoint close-up of 'Nottingham' engraving.

Pairpoint 10.25" #1629 single light candlestick. Crystal with 'Nottingham' engraving: $800-850 pair. Look carefully to find the giant tear-drop shape inside the column.

Pairpoint alternate view of 'Nottingham' engraving.

Pairpoint close-up of 'Grapes' engraving.

Pairpoint 10.5" #1600 single light candle holder. Amethyst with 'Grapes' engraving: $800-850 pair. Ground pontil. **Note**: The #1600 is listed in 8", 9", 10", 12", 14", and 16". The height varies from 8" to 16.875".

Pairpoint 10.625" #1600 single light candle holder. Aurora (amber): $425-475 pair.

Right:
Pairpoint 10.75" #1600 single light candle holder with 'Osirus' engraving. Green: $775-850 pair.

Left:
Pairpoint close-up of 'Osirus' engraving.

Left:
Pairpoint 10" #1600 single light candlestick. Crystal with unidentified engraving: $650-700 pair.

Pairpoint alternate view.

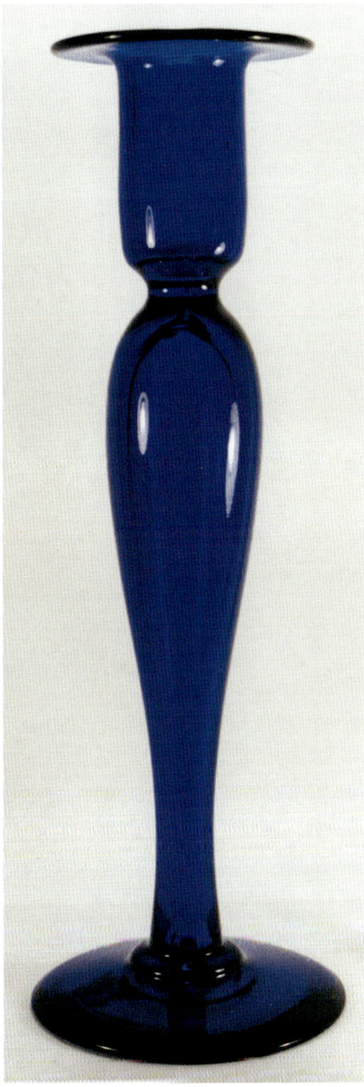

Pairpoint 11.875" #1600 single light candlestick. Cobalt: $600-650 pair. The glass is thick for engraving and cutting and has a ground pontil.

Above left:
Pairpoint 11.875" #1600 single light candlestick. Crystal with 'Wickham' engraving: $775-850 pair.

Above right:
Pairpoint alternate view of 'Wickham' engraving.

Left:
Pairpoint close-up of 'Wickham' engraving.

Pairpoint 12" #1811 variation single light candle stick. Green: $500-550 pair. The base is thick glass for engraving and cutting and has a pontil mark. The candle holder can be found with a thinner domed base and may have prisms.

Pairpoint 12" #B-1627 single light bubble ball stem candle holder. Green/crystal: $475-525 pair.

Right:
Pairpoint 13.75" #1812 'Veneti' design spiral single light candlestick. Crystal with red and white spiral and 'Rockford' engraving on light and base: $1550-1650 pair. This pattern is found on most 'Veniti' pieces.

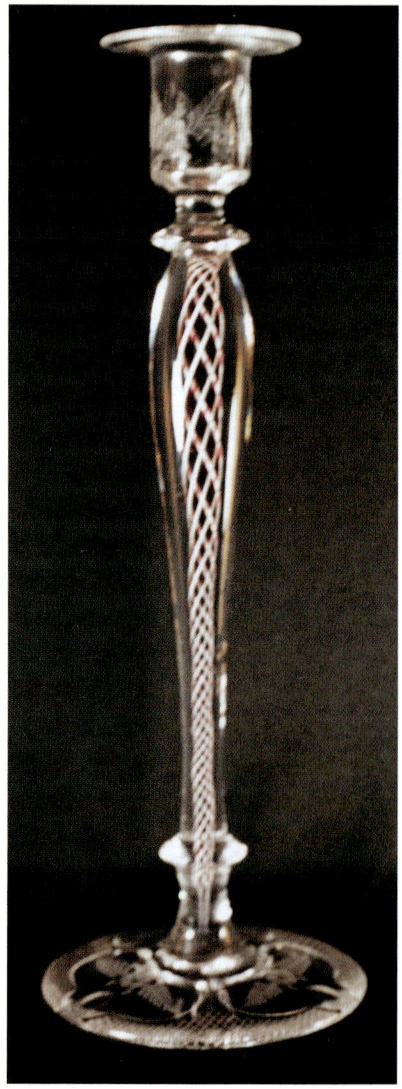

Pairpoint close-up of spiral and 'Rockford' engraving on cup.

Pairpoint close-up of 'Rockford' engraving with cabochon medallions and crosshatching on base.

Pitkin & Brooks

Chicago, Illinois, 1872-1920. Maintained various glass businesses in Indiana. Brilliant cut glass. Acted as a large distributor for the midwest.

Pitkin & Brooks 7.5" 'Imported Candlestick Blank' single light candle holder with panel and diamond balls. Crystal with diamond field cutting: $350-400 pair. Also comes in 9.25" and 10.5". (c. Early 1900s).

Portland Glass Company

Portland, Maine, 1863-1873. Pressed tableware and novelties. Best known pattern is "Tree of Life Group."

Portland 7" 'Portland' or 'Plain Portland' colonial style single light skirted candle holder/vase. Vaseline: $300-350 pair. The skirt on these candle holders can be found with varying degrees of flaring or cupping and heights will vary accordingly. The molds were acquired by **U.S. Glass**.

Portland 7" 'Portland' or 'Plain Portland' single light skirted candle holder/vase. Crystal: $275-300 pair. Can be found with various cuttings which will increase the price.

H.P. Sinclair and Company

Corning, New York, 1904-1928. Cut and engraved glassware. Full lines, lamps, candelabra, and chandeliers. Colored and cased glass after 1920.

Before 1920, **Sinclair** purchased most of its blanks from other suppliers. Major suppliers were **Dorflinger & Sons**, **Corning Glass Works**, and **Pairpoint Corporation**. Minor suppliers included **Baccarat**, **Webb**, **Steuben**, **Libbey**, **Westmoreland**, and **Duncan & Miller**. After 1920, **Sinclair** made most of its own blanks, as well as some for **Steuben**.

Sinclair 3.375" x 4.625" roll edge style single light candle holder with floral engraving on top ring. Colonial blue: $350-375 pair; gold (amber), crystal: $275-300 pair. (c. 1920s). Marked on base.

Below:
Sinclair 10.125" #12927 single light candlestick. Amber: **$**500-550 pair. (c. 1920s).

Sinclair 7.75" #2925 single light candlestick. Crystal/cobalt with floral engraving on candle cup and base: $400-425 pair. (c. 1910s-1920s).

Sabino

Sabino 10.25" single light candle holder. Crystal opalescent with large drip circle: $600-650 pair.

Steuben

Corning, New York, 1903-present. Colored glass and art glass, 1903-1933; contemporary cut and engraved colorless glass, 1933-present. **Steuben** colors were made until 1933 after which they were phased out and only crystal or "colorless" glass was made

Sinclair 11.875" #12900 optic ribbed single light candle holder. Colonial blue: $550-600 pair; light olive: $500-550 pair. (c. 1924-1927).

Steuben 2.5" hand blown reeded single light candle holder. Bristol yellow: $250-275 pair.

Steuben 6.125" heavy single light candle holder with tear drop. Crystal: $750-800 pair.

Steuben 8.75" #7792 'Teardrop' single light candle holder with domed base. Crystal: $1000-1200 pair.

Steuben 10" single light candle holder. Marina blue: $500-550 pair. (c. 1920s).

Steuben 10.125" #3178 single light candle holder. 'Verre de Soie' (iridized lead glass) with applied deep pink edges and 'Waverly' engraving: $1500-1700 pair. (c. 1920s). Also made in various colors and in cased lead glass with or without the circular drip plate.

Steuben 9.75" #2956 single light ribbed candle holder. Aquamarine: $550-600 pair; amber topaz, celeste blue: $500-550 pair. Can be found in several color combinations such as amber topaz/Flemish blue. Also made in 12". Also found plain with no rib pattern and in a combination of a ribbed cup and base with a plain column.

Steuben close-up of wafer and candle cup.

Steuben 10.25" #3178 single light ribbed candle holder. Dark blue/ crystal: $1000-1200 pair. (c. 1920s). Can be found optic-ribbed and in other colors.

Right:
Steuben 12" #6110 single light ribbed candle holder with 'Basketweave' pattern. Pomona green: $700-750 pair. (c. 1920s). Can be found in various colors and treatments and in ribbed or optic-ribbed.

Steuben close-up of 'Basketweave' pattern on drip plate.

Tiffany

Tiffany 8.25" single light candle holder with three dolphins. Lead crystal: $200-225 pair. Marked 'Tiffany & Co'. These sticks are very heavy.

Tiffany close-up of dolphins.

United States Glass Company/Tiffin

Pittsburgh, Pennsylvania, 1891-1938. Moved main office to Tiffin, Ohio; from 1951-1969, **Tiffin Glass** was the only remaining factory; 1980 was the final year of production. Dinnerware lines.

Tiffin 'Autumn Leaf' console set with 1.625" #10 single light candle holders and 12" #319 bowl. Frosted pink with leaf design: candle holders: $60-65 pair; bowl: $80-85 each; set: $140-150. **Note**: The decoration is applied to the undersides of the items; gold is added to the top and sides. This decoration was furnished on pink satin only. (1926-1935).

Tiffin close-up of 'Autumn Leaf' decoration.

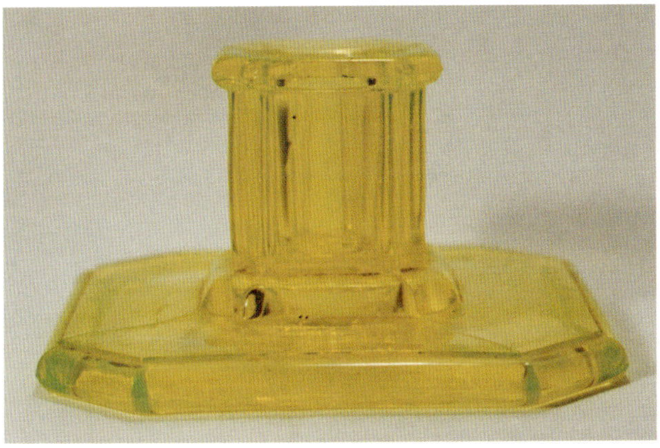

Tiffin 2.25" #18 single light candle holder. Canary, green, blue, pink, black, amber, crystal: bright finish: $45-50 pair; satin finish: $55-60 pair. (1926-1939).

U.S. Glass 3.125" 'Puritan' single light candle holder. Crystal with floral cutting: $35-40 pair; crystal, crystal satin: $30-35 pair. (c. 1926-1931). We have seen this candle holder in crystal only. Can be found with stain on base and cut to clear; also found with decoration under base.

U.S. Glass 3.25" x 5.125" #93 single light candle holder. Green satin with 'Sweet Pea' decoration (one of the most popular during this time), pink satin with decoration: $70-75 pair. (1926-1935). Made in pink and green satin only.

U.S. Glass close-up of cutting.

U.S. Glass close-up of decoration.

U.S. Glass 3.5" x 4.375" #5831 'Athens-Diana' single light candle holder. Crystal with 'Diana' etching and 'Athens' platinum encrusted decorative band: $115-125 pair; Mandarin (a beautiful amber) with gold encrusted 'Athens' decoration: $140-150 pair. (1931-1937). This candle holder with etching, but without gold or silver decoration, was called 'Diana' (1929-1935). Crystal: $75-80 pair; Mandarin: $95-100 pair.

Tiffin 4.25" single light dolphin candle holders. Pink, green, blue: $95-100 pair.

Tiffin 4.25" single light dolphin candle holders. Green: $95-100 pair. Note the plain base.

U.S. Glass close-up of 'Diana' etching with 'Athens' platinum decoration.

Left:
Tiffin 4.25" single light dolphin candle holders. Pink, blue: $95-100 pair.

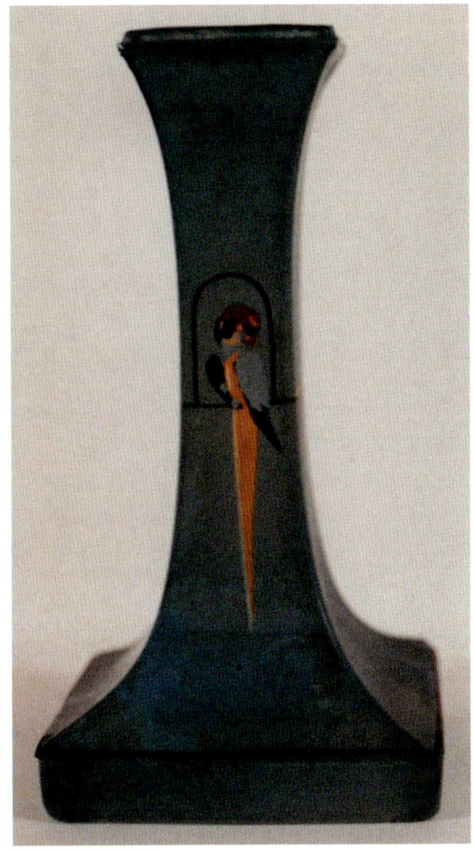

U.S. Glass 5.625" 'Jungle Assortment' single light candle holder with #14 'Parrot' decoration. Crystal with blue paint, crystal, crystal satin, crystal with green paint, crystal with orange paint, crystal with canary paint, two different blues: $65-70 pair; green satin: $75-80 pair. (c. 1922-1934).

Tiffin 4.25" and 7.5" single light dolphin candle holders shown for size comparison. Pink, green, blue: 4.25": $95-100 pair; 7.5": $195-200 pair.

Tiffin 5.125" #72 'Frog' single light candle holders. Black satin, black opaque: $275-300 pair. (c. 1920s-1930s).

Tiffin 6.5" #79 single light candle holder. Canary: $80-85 pair; amber, crystal: $55-60 pair; amber satin, crystal satin: $60-65 pair; blue, pink, green, amethyst, black: $65-70 pair; black satin, royal blue satin, ruby: $95-100 pair; black with 'Echec' (geometric design combining opaque and satin): $115-125 pair. (c. 1926-1940s). Possibly found in other satin colors.

U.S. Glass 7" #77 hexagonal single light candle holder with skirted base. Canary satin, canary: $70-75 pair; crystal: $50-55 pair; sky blue: $80-85 pair. (c. 1926-1929). Can be found with various colors of painted bodies on crystal and with various decorations. Probably found in other colors.

Tiffin 7.5" #6101 single light candle holder with hexagonal stem. Tiffin rose (pink), twilight (light amethyst), crystal with cobalt candle bowl: $200-210 pair; plum (amethyst), golden banana (yellow): $135-145 pair. Can be found with #6102 'Diamond Optic' hurricane shade: add $60-65 each. Golden banana and plum 1945-1963; all others 1962-1963.

U.S. Glass 6.5" #56 Colonial style single light candle holder with hex-oval base. Crystal with silver decoration: $70-75 pair. (c. 1920s).

U.S. Glass 7.5" G#15140 four-sided single light candle holder. Crystal with Greek key silver decoration: $150-175 pair. (c. 1919). 'G' denotes the **Gillander & Sons** factory in Greensburg, Pennsylvania. Shown in a 1919 export catalog for Mexico and South America. Very good quality glass.

Tiffin 8.25" #151 skirted single light candle holder. Crystal with cobalt blue paint and unidentified gold overlay, orange paint, and various silver overlay decorations: $95-100 pair; black, black satin, royal blue satin (all with various decorations): $125-135 pair; crystal, crystal satin: $90-100 pair; blue iridescent, canary iridescent: $130-140 pair; pink iridescent: $165-175 pair; ruby (amberina) with decoration: $190-200 pair. (c. 1924-1934).

Tiffin alternate view of gold overlay pattern.

Tiffin alternate view of gold overlay pattern.

Tiffin 8.375" #151 single light candle holder. Crystal with vertical cuttings and punties with unidentified gold encrusted plate etching: $190-200 pair. (c. 1920s).

U.S. Glass 8.5" x 4.25" #151 single light candle holder. Opaque colors: coral red: $175-185 pair; jade green, pearl blue: $150-160 pair. (Introduced in 1921). Two-part mold.

Tiffin close-up of gold decoration.

U.S. Glass 8.375" #76 single light candle holder. Emerald green satin with enameled floral hand decoration and gold trim: $110-125 pair; light green, green, sapphire blue: $80-85 pair; crystal, crystal satin: $70-80 pair; black, black satin: $120-130 pair; sky blue, sky blue satin, royal blue, royal blue satin: $140-150 pair. (c. 1920s). All may be found with various decorations and will command higher prices.

U.S. Glass close-up of decoration.

U.S. Glass alternate view of decoration.

U.S. Glass console set with 8.375" #76 single light candle holders and 10.25" #15179 footed floral compote. Emerald green satin with hand decorations: $170-185 set. (c. 1920s).

Tiffin 8.125" #66 spiral or twist single light candlestick. Satin colors: dark amber, crystal: $60-65 pair; canary, reflex green, sky blue: $75-80 pair; amberina, amethyst, emerald green: $80-90 pair; black: $95-100 pair; royal blue: $100-110 pair; jasper (opaque pinkish tan): $140-150 pair. Transparent colors: dark amber, crystal: $55-60 pair; reflex green, sky blue: $70-75 pair; amethyst, emerald green: $80-85 pair; black: $90-95 pair; royal blue: $95-100 pair. (c. 1920s). Listed as 7.5", but varies from 7.5" to 8.25".

Above left:
U.S. Glass 8.5" #76 single light candle holder. Amethyst with enameled floral and gold decoration: $95-100 pair. (c. 1920s).

Above right:
Tiffin 8.25" #66 spiral or twist single light candlestick. Amberina: $80-85 pair. (c. 1920s). Three-part mold; the similar **Cambridge** mold is two-part.

Left:
U.S. Glass 8.625" #76 single light candle holder. Light green with silver floral overlay and silver edges: $95-100 pair. (c. 1920s).

Right:
Tiffin 8.5" #300 single light candlestick. Crystal with cobalt blue paint and unidentified silver overlay: $95-100 pair; amber satin without decoration: $100-110 pair; royal blue satin, black satin, green satin (all without decoration): $115-125 pair. See the 8.25" crystal with cobalt #151 on p. 157 for a close-up of the overlay decoration. (c. 1920s).

Tiffin 8.5" #80 single light open twisted candle holders. Crystal with ruby stain: $115-125 pair; crystal: $85-90 pair; royal blue, blue, amethyst, amber, white milk glass, jasper (opaque pinkish tan): $100-110 pair. These have been drilled to be used as lamp bases. (c. 1920s).

Right:
U.S. Glass 8.75" single light candle holder. Amber: $65-75 pair; canary, canary satin: $85-95 pair. These are the only two colors we have seen for this stick, but there are probably others.

Far left:
U.S. Glass 8.625" #50 single light candle holder. Crystal with gold outlines and ruby stain on bottom of column: $150-175 pair. (c. 1919). This candle holder has been cut top and bottom. Shown in a 1919 export catalog for Mexico and South America from 'F' factory, which was the old **Ripley & Co.** at Pittsburgh, Pennsylvania. Very good quality glass.

Left:
Tiffin 9" #15310 or #310 single light candle holder. Crystal, crystal satin: $85-95 pair; pink: $95-100 pair; green, black, amberina: $100-125 pair. (c. 1922-1935). The number was changed to #310 in the 1920s. Tiffin made a 'Holly Satin Assortment' that included a red satin and a green satin.

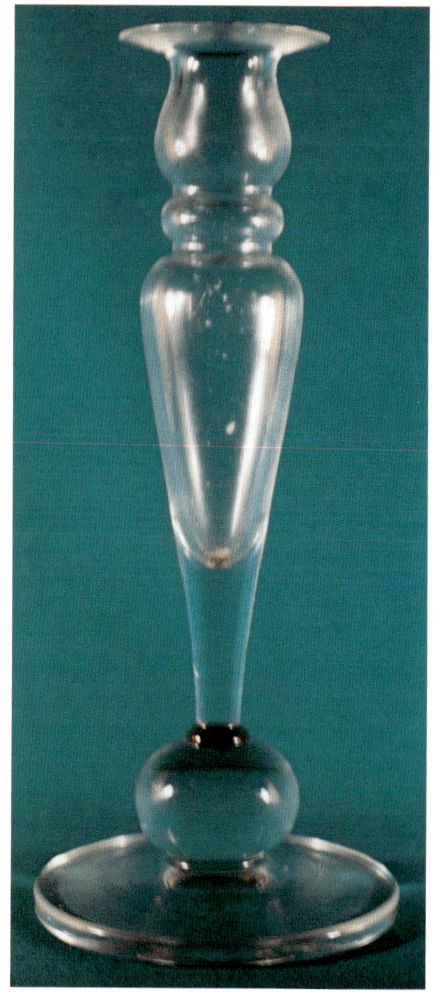

Left:
Tiffin 9.375" #310 single light candle holder. Canary opaline stretch: $140-150 pair; blue stretch: $125-135 pair; green opaline stretch: $175-185 pair. (c. 1922-1935).

Right:
Tiffin 9.5" single light smooth candle/vase with solid ball at base. Crystal: $225-250 pair.

Tiffin 9.375" #310 single light candle holder. Amber satin, amber: $85-95 pair; green satin, pink satin, black satin, amberina satin: $110-135 pair. (c. 1922-1935).

Left:
Tiffin 9.375" #310 single light candle holder. Canary: $95-100 pair; canary satin: $100-115 pair; canary stretch: $125-135 pair. (c. 1922-1935).

Right:
Tiffin 9.75" #179 single light bell base twist candle holder. Sky blue, canary: $110-120 pair; crystal: $95-100 pair; amberina: $145-155 pair. (c. 1920s-1930s).

Tiffin 9.75" #179 single light bell base twist candle holders. Canary stretch, sky blue stretch: $165-175 pair; canary satin, sky blue satin: $125-135 pair; crystal satin: $100-110 pair; crystal stretch (mother-of-pearl): $135-145 pair; amberina satin: $155-165 pair. (c. 1920s-1930s).

Tiffin 9.875" and 10" #319 single light candle holders. Sky blue satin, emerald green satin, black satin: $140-150 pair; crystal, amber: $85-90 pair; crystal satin, amber satin: $90-100 pair; canary: $115-125 pair; canary satin, sky blue, emerald green, black: $125-135 pair; amberina: $145-155 pair; amberina satin: $155-165 pair. (c. 1920s-1930s). Can be found with various decorations and will command higher prices.

Tiffin 10" #319 single light candle holder. Canary satin: $125-135 pair.

Tiffin console with 10" single light candle holders and 11" bowl. Emerald green satin: $200-225 set.

Left:
Tiffin 10" #319 single light candle holder. Emerald green satin: $140-150 pair.

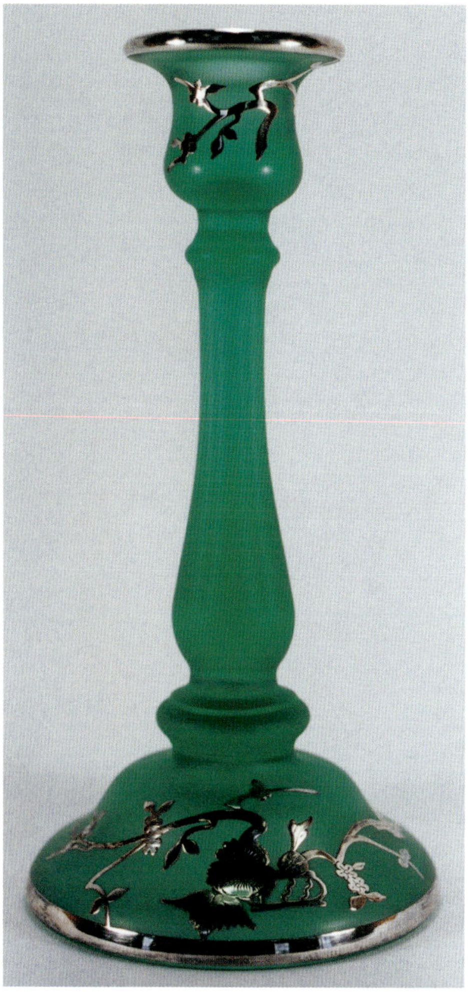

Left:
Tiffin 10" #84 single light candle holder. Green satin with silver 'Kobi Basket' overlay: $185-195 pair; without decoration: crystal, amber: $70-75 pair; crystal satin, amber satin: $75-80 pair; canary: $95-100 pair; canary satin: $100-110 pair; sky blue, black, emerald green: $120-130 pair; sky blue satin, black satin, emerald green satin: $135-145 pair; opaque pinkish brown: $165-170 pair. (c. 1920s). All can be found with various decorations and will command higher prices. Possibly found in other known **Tiffin** colors.

Right:
Tiffin 5" #15360 double light candle holder with 'Coronet' plate etching: $95-100 pair. Can be found with various etchings and cuttings.

Tiffin close-up of plate etching.

U.S. Glass 12" #61 single light candle pillar. Crystal: $225-250 pair. Found in the 1919 catalog from factory 'F', **Old Ripley & Co.**, Pittsburgh, Pennsylvania. Very good quality glass.

Tiffin 1.75" x 14.5" x 9.5" #5905-20 with lily pond (#5905) and 10" 'Fawn' (#6322) triple light candle/flower floater. Crystal: $150-175 set; citron: $300-325 set; copen blue: $375-400 set. **Note**: Has been reissued in vaseline to a private individual by **Summit Art Glass Co.** which now owns the mold.

Tiffin close-up of #6322 'Fawn'.

Westmoreland Specialty Company

Grapeville, Pennsylvania, 1889-1984. Milk glass and giftware.

Westmoreland 3" x 6.5" #10 'Lotus' line #1921 single light candle holder. Bermuda blue, golden sunset, apricot mist: $45-50 pair; green mist, olive green, light blue mist: $40-45 pair; pink opalescent: $50-55 pair; flame (amberina): $60-65 pair. (c. 1960s). Flame and golden sunset hard to find.

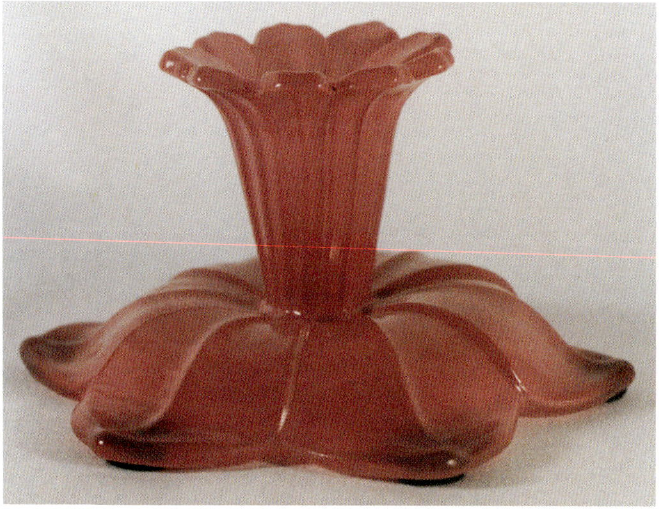

Westmoreland 3.25" x 5.5" #2 'Lotus' line #1921 single light candle holder. Rose-lavender spray cased (c. 1975), any spray cased color: $115-125 pair; green mist, dark blue mist, light blue mist, mother-of-pearl, crystal mist, pink mist: $70-75 pair; apricot mist, lilac mist: $80-85 pair; black satin: $85-90 pair; crystal with ruby stain: $100-110 pair. 'Mist' indicates satin glass. (c. 1920s intermittently until 1984).

Westmoreland 3.375" x 4.25" #1067 'Three Ball' with #L-130 'King's Jewels' decoration single light candle holder with base. Crystal with champagne and ruby stained balls, crystal with burgundy (replaced later by ruby), champagne and green luster staining: $70-75 pair; crystal: $55-60 pair. This is the original mold (1927-1940); for a very short time (1940), it was available with or without the base. The later mold (#1067/1, c. 1940-?) without the base is found more often: with lustre: $60-65 pair; without lustre: $45-50 pair.

Westmoreland 3.75" x 5" #2 'Lotus' line #1921single light candle holder. White milk glass, moss green, golden sunset: $65-70 pair; black milk glass, pink-lilac pastel, pink opalescent, light blue pastel: $80-85 pair; flame: $120-130 pair. (c. 1920s intermittently until 1984).

Westmoreland 3.25" x 4.25" #1058 'Della Robia' single light candle holder. Crystal with luster stained fruits: $70-75 pair; crystal: $55-60 pair. (c. 1928-1940s).

Westmoreland 3.875" #20 'Paneled Grape' line #1881 single light candle holder. Black milk glass, almond milk glass, brandywine blue, laurel green, crystal velvet (crystal with frosted pattern): $45-50 pair; white milk glass: $30-35 pair; white milk glass mother-of-pearl, golden sunset: $35-40 pair; crystal with ruby stain: $55-60 pair; white milk glass with decorations: 22K gold: $40-45 pair; 'Green & Gold' decoration #86: $50-55 pair; hand painted fruit #85: $70-75 pair; 'Roses & Bows' decoration #32: $90-95 pair.

Westmoreland 4.25" x 4.125" #3 'Scroll & Lace' line #1872 single light candle holder. White milk glass with gold decoration: $65-70 pair. (c. 1960s). Marked. Early 1900s versions are usually white milk glass or crystal mist; older versions with decorations are scarce.

Westmoreland 4.25" x 4.125" #3 'Scroll & Lace' line #1872 single light candle holder. White milk glass with holly decoration: $85-90 pair; crystal mist or any **Westmoreland** color without decoration: $45-50 pair. (c. 1970s). Marked. Reissued by **Westmoreland** in several colors. The mold is currently owned by **Summit Art Glass**.

Westmoreland 4" #1 'Dolphin' line #1409 single light candle holders. Almond milk glass: $40-45 pair, black milk glass, pink pastel: $45-50 pair; white milk glass, crystal: $30-35 pair; crystal mist: $35-40 pair; almond mist, antique blue, antique blue mist: $40-45 pair. (c. 1950-1984). Marked. Reissued by **Dalzell** as #1937 in other colors.

Westmoreland alternate view of "marriage" pieces. 'Wakefield' fairy light globe: $40-45 each; #3 'Wedding Bowl' candle holder: $35-40 each; **Clark** 'Fairy Lite' peg: $25-30 each.

Westmoreland and **Clark** "marriage" of 4.5" **Westmoreland** 'Wedding Bowl' base, 4.25" **Westmoreland** 'Wakefield' fairy light globe, and a **Clark** 1.375" x 4" 'Fairy Lite' peg. This is one of many marriages (pattern or manufacturer combinations) we have found that we wanted to share. This does make a beautiful presentation.

Westmoreland 4.5" x 3.25" 'Wedding Bowl' single light candle holder. Crystal with ruby stain: $75-80 pair; white milk glass, crystal: $35-40 pair; crystal with ruby stain with white roses painted on top of stain, white milk glass with decoration: $90-95 pair. (c. 1930s-early 1980s). Hard to find in crystal or with any decoration.

Westmoreland 4.75" #3 'Doric' line #23 single light candle holder. Flame (amberina), ruby, lilac, lilac opalescent, black: $55-60 pair; golden sunset, amber, yellow mist, white milk glass: $30-35 pair; apricot, blue pastel, pink pastel, crystal mist, moss green, dark blue mist, light blue mist, green mist: $35-40 pair; almond, almond mist, green, pink mist, Bermuda blue, laurel green, mint green, mint green mist: $40-45 pair. Marked.

Westmoreland 'Princess Feather' line #201 table center with 3.25" single light candle holders and 8" x 10.5" banana bowl. Rose amber: $75-85 set. Note that the 'Doric' candle holder is used for the base of the bowl.

Westmoreland 4.875" #9 'American Hobnail' line #77 single light candle holder. Brandywine blue opalescent: $70-75 pair; white milk glass: $35-40 pair; lilac opalescent: $60-65 pair; candlelight (moonstone): $65-70 pair. Milk glass candle holders were produced mainly in the 1950s, opalescents in the 1970s.

Left:
Westmoreland 4.875" #1 'Maple Leaf' line #1928 single light candle holder with flat top. White milk glass; $40-45 pair; mint green opaque (c. 1979): $75-80 pair. Introduced in 1920s as 'Bramble' in white milk glass and again in 1950s as 'Maple Leaf'. Also found with a crimped top (c. 1981-1984) in transparent colors: blue pastel (sapphire), pink pastel: $50-55 pair; lilac opalescent, ruby: $80-85 pair. Reissued by **Plum Glass**.

Right:
Westmoreland 5.25" x 4.125" #9 'Ashburton' line #1855 single light candle holder with six-paneled base. Olive green, moss green, amber, golden sunset, crystal: $30-35 pair; Bermuda blue: $35-40 pair; crystal with ruby stain: $60-65 pair. (Produced in 1940s, 1950s and 1970s).

Left:
Westmoreland 7" #54 crucifix single light candle holder. Crystal with gold decoration, white milk glass with gold decoration: $150-175 pair. (c. early 1900s).

Right:
Westmoreland 7.375" #1012 single light four-paneled candlestick. Crystal with vertical cuts and solid base, black plain: $80-85 pair. (c. 1915-1940). Various cuttings will command higher prices. Also made in 8".

Right:
Westmoreland 7.375" #1010 single light candle holder with hexagonal base, column and round rim candle cup. Crystal with vertical 'Bead and Reel' notching and unknown cutting: $70-75 pair; amber with no cutting: $60-65 pair. (c. late 1920s-1930s). Possibly made in other colors. Three other companies had a similar mold; all have a hexagonal candle cup rim. **Jeanette's** #97 candle holder is thinner; **Lancaster's** candle cup is shorter and more flared; and **Heisey's** candle holder is made of superior glass.

Far right:
Westmoreland close-up of cutting.

Westmoreland close-up of cutting.

Westmoreland 7.625" #1016 'Art Nouveau' six-sided, handled single light candle pillar with cutting. Crystal only: with cutting: $140-150 pair; without cutting: $115-125 pair. (c. 1911-1940). Also made in 8". This is the #1019 with handles added.

Westmoreland 7.375" #1023 single light candle holder. Crystal with cutting, black plain: $60-65 pair; crystal plain: $35-40 pair. Available in crystal and colors (1915-1925); crystal only (1932-1940). Most often found plain. Found with two plunger styles, a blunt plunger, and a shortened, pointed one; the outside of the stick is the same. Several companies made a similar candle holder; the ridges on **Westmoreland's** candle cup are exactly 1.125" apart from center to center.

Westmoreland 8" #1002 Doric column style single light candle holder. Crystal with orange spray casing and black decoration: $75-80 pair. (c. 1920s). This candle holder came in crystal only with various decorations (c. 1920s-1930s). Also made in 6.5".

Westmoreland console with 8" #1002 Doric column style single light candle holders and 11.25" #1909/2 bowl on black glass stand. Crystal with yellow and black spray casing on underside and floral hand decoration with gold accents on top surface: candle holders: $100-110 pair; #1909/2 bowl: $55-60 each; bowl stand: $25-30 each. (c. 1920s).

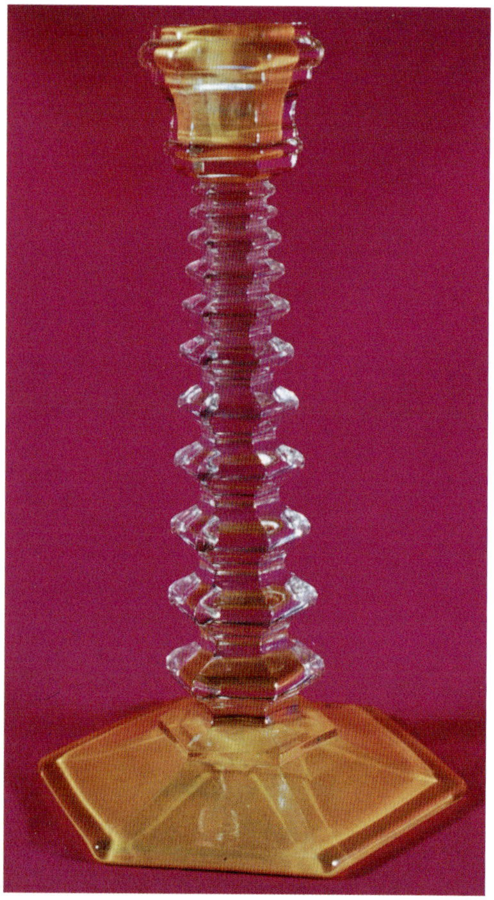

Westmoreland 8" #1017 'Mt. Vernon' single light candle holder. Crystal with yellow-gold spray cased base and candle cup, amber: $95-100 pair. (c. 1920s-1970). Can be found with decorations and possibly other colors. Used as a lamp base in the 1920s.

Westmoreland 8" #130 'English Hobnail' line #555 single light candle holder. Turquoise: $100-110 pair; crystal, white milk glass: $60-65 pair; roselin, green, light blue mist, blue pastel, pink pastel, pink mist: $85-90 pair; lilac opalescent: $125-135 pair; ruby: $150-160 pair. (c. 1925-1970s).

Westmoreland 8.75" #1041 single light candle holder. Crystal only with oxidized silver on all edges and base with enamel colors overlapping the silver circles: $95-100 pair. (c. 1920s). Can be found with several different decorations of this kind.

Left:
Westmoreland 9.25" #1042 single light candle holder. Crystal with hand painted floral decoration under base: $95-100 pair.

Westmoreland close-up of decoration.

Right:
Westmoreland 8.875" #1042 single light candle holder. Belgian blue (introduced in 1931): $120-130 pair; crystal: $70-75 pair; emerald green, green, amber, roselin: $95-100 pair. (c. 1920s-1940s). Can be found with various cuttings, treatments and decorations. Also made in 6.5".

Far right:
Westmoreland 9.125" #1042 'Graceful Scroll' single light candlestick. Crystal with yellow stain and cut-to-clear with etched scallops: $140-150 pair. (c. 1925). Part of Fort Dearborn's 'Graceful Scroll' console set. Also made in 6.5".

Westmoreland 9.25" #1042 single light candlestick. Crystal with heavy gold encrusted plate etching: $95-100 pair. (c. 1920s-1940).

Westmoreland 8.875" #1042 single light candlestick. Emerald green with floral cutting: $110-120 pair.

Westmoreland close-up of gold plate etching.

Westmoreland 9.5" #4 'Dolphin' line #1049 single light candle holders. Antique blue, antique blue mist, almond, blue opalescent, black milk glass: $160-175 pair; crystal satin, pink satin, blue satin, light pink, light blue: $95-100 pair; white milk glass, crystal: $125-135 pair; amber, green, roselin, blue: $190-200 pair. (c. 1924-1984). Also used as a lamp base. Has been reproduced.

Below:
Westmoreland 5.25" x 11.625" #1932/2 'Bowl with Elephant Candle holders' one-piece console set. Ruby carnival: $150-175 each; crystal: $100-125 each; teal blue and other colors: $140-150 each. (c. 1932-1937). *Reproduced* in cobalt and black: $95-100 each.

Below:
Westmoreland 9.25" #1042 single light candle holder. Pink and black spray cased with enameled floral and gold decoration: $150-160 pair.

Westmoreland console set with 9.25" #1042 single light candle holders and 11.5" #1820 footed bowl. Pink and black spray cased and floral and gold decoration: $210-225 set.

Westmoreland 4.25" #1013/1 triple light child's mini 'Candelabra'. Apricot mist, any mist color: $65-70 pair; crystal, blue pastel, pink pastel: $45-50 pair; lavender, ruby (c. 1960s-1980s): $65-70 pair. *Reproduced* in vaseline, crystal, and white milk glass.

Westmoreland 5.25" x 8.25" #26 Line #1921 'Lotus' triple light candle holder. Pink Mist (c. 1950s), light blue mist, green mist, milk glass: $95-100 pair; crystal, crystal mist: $75-80 pair; any spray cased color combination: $150-165 pair. Introduced in 1920s; reissued in 1950s.

Westmoreland alternate view.